18 Projects to Sew Through the Seasons

Lovely Little Patchwork

Kerri Horsley

Tuva Publishing

www.tuvapublishing.com

Address: Merkez Mah. Cavusbasi Cad. No:71
Cekmekoy - Istanbul 34782 / Turkey
Tel: +9 0216 642 62 62

Lovely Little Patchwork

First Print: 2016 / February

All Global Copyrights Belongs To
Tuva Tekstil ve Yayıncılık Ltd

Content: Patchwork

Editor in Chief: Ayhan DEMİRPEHLİVAN
Project Editor: Kader DEMİRPEHLİVAN
Designer: Kerri HORSLEY
Technical Editor: K. Leyla ARAS, Büşra ESER
Assistant: Zilal ÖNEL
Graphic Design: Ömer ALP, Abdullah BAYRAKÇI
Photography: Kerri HORSLEY, Tuva Publishing
Illustrations: Murat Tanhu YILMAZ
Place of the photography: CafeCraftIstanbul

ISBN: 978-605-9192-06-4

Printing House
Bilnet Matbaacılık ve Yayıncılık A.Ş.

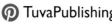

TuvaYayincilik   TuvaPublishing
TuvaYayincilik   TuvaPublishing

Contents

Projects

Preface

I was raised in Seattle, Washington, and ever since childhood I have loved crafting and sewing. As a young girl I remember going to my Aunts' homes and admiring the lovely works of art that they had created! They were true inspirations for me and helped shape my creative side. My Aunt Paula, would spend (and still does) hours sewing hexagons and working on embroidery. My Aunt Terri also creates the most beautiful embroidery work. I remember going to my Aunt Beth's house as she would help alter our clothes so they would fit 'just right'. I had a close friend whose mom had a large sewing room and remember thinking that some day I would have a sewing room when I grew up. I also give credit to my loving parents who always supported me in my hopes and dreams. With the desire to create, they steered me in the right direction by having me take sewing lessons as a teenager. Soon after starting my lessons, I received my first sewing machine for Christmas and was so excited to have my very own. Being able to sew a simple skirt or holiday decoration was so gratifying. To this day I still have one of the holiday decorations I stitched from one of my sewing lessons. I married my high school sweet heart and we have 6 wonderful children. I love being able to sew and craft with my kids. Sewing pillowcases, little stuffed animals, or holiday decorations, I'm hoping to pass these traditions and love for creating onto them.

As an adult, I was introduced to quilting from my sweet mother-in-law and sister-in-law, and once I started, I was hooked. Soon after starting to quilt I began writing about my sewing adventures on my blog "Lovely Little Handmades". I was able to get involved online through Flickr and started organizing swaps with a sweet and spunky friend, Heather of "House of Alamode" and "Citizens of Textile". We did swap groups for out-of-print fabric, pillows, home goods, embroidery, and seasonal/holiday items. A network of friends blossomed as I was able to get more involved. I truly adore the quilting and crafting community. The support and love they give is endless.

I have a deep love for pretty vintage fabrics, vintage embroidery and lovely reproductions, especially, in bright colors like aqua, pink, red and yellow. I love thrifting and always search for vintage fabrics, buttons, quilts, and supplies. It truly makes my heart flutter when I find a treasure that has been lost and forgotten.

Sewing small patchwork projects has become one of my favorites. Creating a smaller item like a pillow is the prefect way to try a new technique. It also gives you a chance to work with different combinations of fabric. By sewing with different fabrics while using a new technique helps you find what truly makes your heart sing. In the summer time I especially love to stitch up something with a strawberry or sailboat. Yet in the fall, it gives me a chance to sew with pretty fall colors (that I may not be drawn to during the other times of the year), and designs like pumpkins or leaves.

I hope in Lovely Little Patchwork you will be inspired to create lovely and pretty things that you can use year after year! Whether you are a novice or advanced sewist, I encourage you to enjoy the process and not worry if something doesn't come out perfect. Handmade items are not about having something perfect, but more about putting your heart into making something that you and your loved ones will cherish over time.

Most of all, Have Fun!!

Kerri Horsley

Basic Patchwork Tools

Making sure you have the right tools for each project is one way you will have ease and enjoyment through the process. Everything listed here can be found easily online or at your local craft store. When going to purchase tools I recommend going with quality. Having higher quality tools may cost a bit more but will be well worth it in the end.

These are the following tools I always have close by and on hand while I work:

✳ Rotary cutter and mat

✳ Ruler (I use many sizes, large, small, different size squares, and triangles)

✳ Scissors (embroidery and fabric)

✳ Ironing board and iron (I prefer vintage irons as they are stainless steel and get really hot which makes for pressing seams easier and more accurate).

✳ Seam ripper

✳ 505 basting spray (temporary fabric adhesive)

✳ Water-soluble pen

✳ Fusible web (double sided)

✳ Thread

✳ Pins and Needles

✳ Pincushion

✳ Embroidery hoop

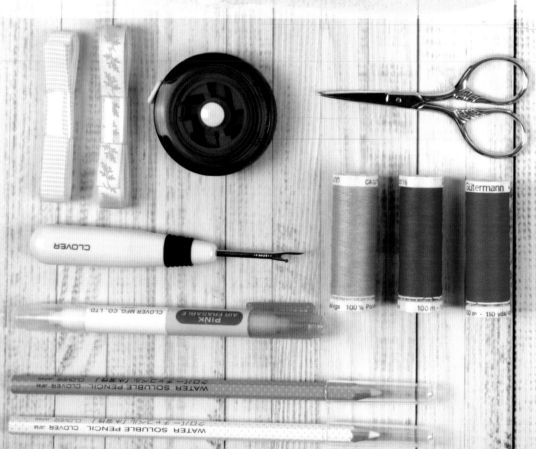

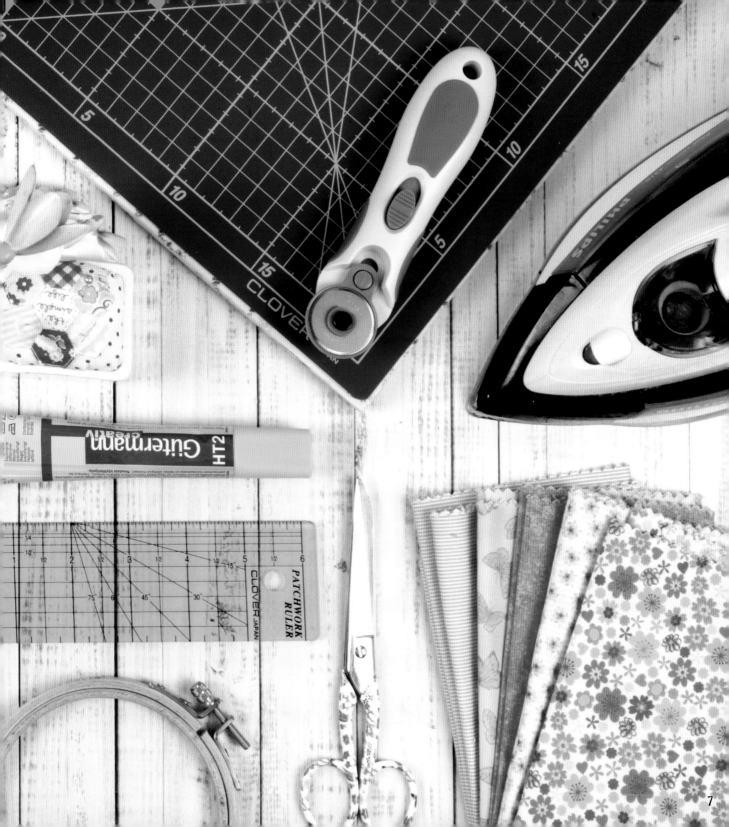

Techniques

Foundation Paper Piecing

Tips on Paper Piecing

It is important when paper piecing to cut your fabric pieces large enough to cover each numbered area. It is best to cut it extra large and then trim your piece and save the scraps for another project. It can be hard to tell the exact size you need so it is better to go larger so you do not have to seam rip it after it is sewn, and then cut a new piece.

Templates are mirrored images of the finished block. Since you're sewing the fabric on the backside of the paper, when the block is finished it will mirror the paper copy image.

A couple great tools for paper piecing are an Add-A-Quarter ruler and a basic envelope. The envelope helps stabilize the paper when you need to fold it back. Then the Add-A-Quarter ruler rests perfectly against the folded paper and envelope so you can trim your pieces to a perfect ¼" (6mm) seam.

Piecing Your Block

1 Place your fabric piece number 1 right side up on the back side of the paper and pin in place. Hold your paper up to a window or light so you can make sure you have positioned it to cover the entire space and it extends at least a ¼" (6mm) on each side. Fold your paper back so you can trim a ¼" (6mm) seam allowance between piece number 1 and 2.

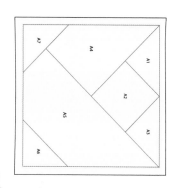

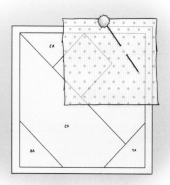

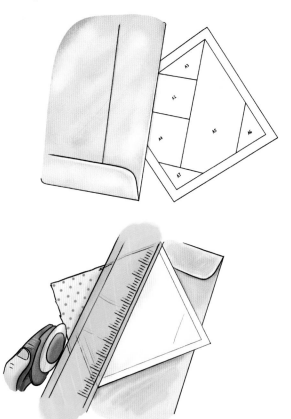

2 Place fabric piece number 2 on top of fabric piece number 1 with right sides together. Make sure your fabric piece number 2 is large enough to extend at least a ¼" (6mm) on all sides.

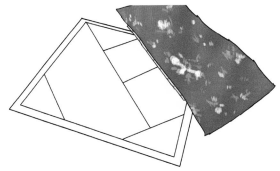

3 Turn your paper over so you see the design. Machine stitch on the line between space number 1 and 2. Backstitch at the beginning and end. Reduce your stitch length. I prefer a pretty small stitch length to help make removing the paper easier later on.

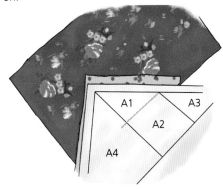

4 Fold your paper back between piece numbers 1 and 2 and trim the excess fabric so the seam allowance is a ¼" (6mm). Press piece number 2 at the seam. Place piece number 3 right sides together along the seam of 2 and 3. Turn your paper over and machine stitch the line between number 2 and 3. Make sure to backstitch at the beginning and end. Trim your seam allowance to a ¼" (6mm) and press piece number 3 at the seam.

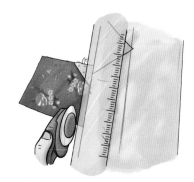

5 Continue adding each piece in numerical order, then trimming and pressing your seams.

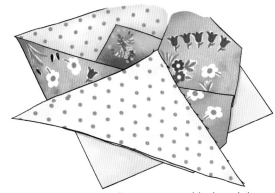

6 Once your block is complete press your block and then trim around all the edges leaving a ¼" (6mm) seam allowance around all sides. Leave your paper attached.

English Paper Piecing

 Paper

 Fabric
Right Side

 Fabric
Wrong Side

 Thread

 Knot

1 Place the hexagon on the wrong side (back) of fabric. Pin in place if preferred. Trim a generous ¼" (6mm) to 3/8" (1cm) around the outside of the hexagon.

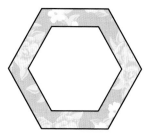

2 Fold the top edge down over the paper hexagon.

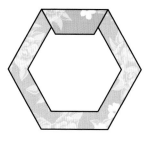

3 To baste your hexagon, take your needle and thread it with the contrasting thread and knot the end of the thread. Insert your needle from the front to back side through the fabric and paper. Your knot will be on the front side.

4 Fold the next edge down over the paper hexagon and insert your needle from back to front through the next corner. Continue going counter clockwise folding down each edge and passing your needle through each corner so all sides are folded over and tacked down.

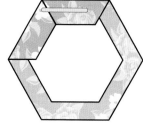

5 When you get to your last corner, your thread should be in the front. Tie your thread in a knot and trim. Continue with steps 1-5 until you have 7 hexagons.

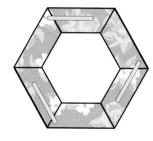

6 Hold two hexagons together with right sides facing. Thread your needle with coordinating thread and knot the end. Insert your needle in the corner of your hexagon going through both hexagons. Use a whipstitch to attach the two hexagons, make close tight stitches along the top edge. Make sure to take only the very edge of the fabric trying not to go through the paper.

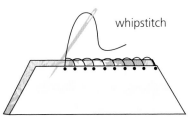

whipstitch

7 Continue attaching hexagons to the center one going counter clockwise using a whipstitch.

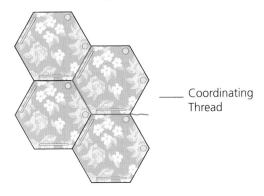

Coordinating Thread

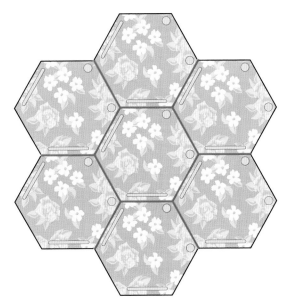

8 After all the sides (flower petals) are attached to the center hexagon, whipstitch the six outside petals one at a time in the same way, right sides together.

9 Once you are ready to attach your flower to your project, iron your grandmother's flower garden and then carefully remove the basting stitches and paper.

Raw Edge Appliqué

Tips on Sketchy Appliqué

One of my favorite types of appliqué is sketchy (raw edge) appliqué. It is an easy way to turn an illustration or picture into a fabric art piece! I typically use dark thread colors that will make the piece pop when appliquéing this method. I also go around each piece twice so the thread shows up and makes the edges more durable. Using double sided fusible web helps secure the pieces in place before you start machine stitching. Keep in mind, when using fusible web the finished project will be in reverse to the pattern.

Instructions

1 Copy all the pattern pieces for the appliqué onto card stock and cut out. Trace the pattern with a pencil onto one of the paper sides of the double sided fusible web.

2 Roughly cut out the pieces leaving at least ¼" around all sides. Peel the paper off the back side of the first piece you are going to work with (the side that doesn't have the pattern drawn on). Place the piece with the paper side up onto the wrong side of the fabric and press. Continue with all the other pieces you will be appliquéing.

3 Cut out the pieces on the drawn pattern lines.

4 Peel the paper off and place the pieces onto the background fabric. Pieces that touch another piece; make sure to overlap them a bit. Press so the appliqué pieces are fused in place. When pressing, set your iron onto the piece for a few seconds, lift the iron and go onto the next area. Try not to go side to side as this can deform the pieces.

5 Thread your machine with dark contrasting thread. I usually use black or navy blue. Start with the under pieces if you are adding layers onto each piece. Stitch around each motif with a short straight stitch going around each motif twice and then press.

Quilting

After you finish a quilt top it is time to layer the quilt with three layers-- the quilt top, batting and backing. I prefer natural cotton batting that can easily be found at craft stores. I typically use vintage sheets for my quilt backs, and cotton prints for my envelope backings on pillows and smaller projects. You can piece the back if you prefer.

Quilt Sandwich

A quilt sandwich is when you create your three layers (quilt top, batting, backing). To keep these layers together you can either pin them together with straight pins, safety pins or quilting basting spray (temporary adhesive spray). I baste with basting spray and include it in many of the directions. It keeps the quilt together more securely and you don't have to worry about puckers on the back when quilting. When I use the quilting spray I lay out a big vintage sheet on the floor (as a floor cover) and place my layers on that so the adhesive doesn't get on the floor.

1   Place the batting piece on the floor cover and then lay the backing right side up on top of the batting.

2   Fold half of the backing back. Hold the basting spray can about 12" (30.5cm) from the batting and spray lightly.

3   Slowly lay the half that was folded back over the batting and press firmly while smoothing out any bumps. Make sure to start from the center when pressing and then go outwards. Fold back the other half of the backing piece and spray baste that side like you just did.

4   Turn the batting over and lay the quilt top right side up on the batting piece. Repeat steps 2 and 3.

If you prefer to use pins, layer the quilt by placing the backing on a hard surface and layer- backing, batting and then quilt top. Pin from the center and moving outwards. Smooth as you go to make sure there are not bumps on the backside. It can be helpful to tape the backing to the hard surface.

Stitching

One of my favorite parts of quilting is stitching the layers together. This is where your quilt truly becomes a quilt. Whether you are free motion quilting, hand quilting, or straight line quilting, it comes to life at this point. If you're doing straight line quilting, this is where you want to use your walking foot, or if you're free motion quilting you'll use a darning foot.

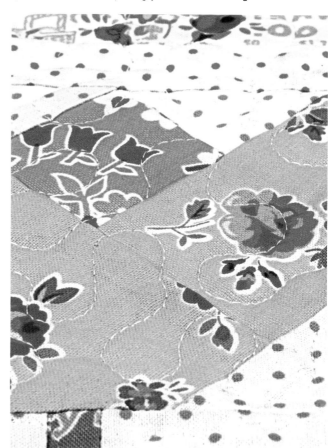

Free Motion Quilting

Free-motion quilting is when you drop your feed dogs and quilt in a free motion design. Stippling is one design where you meander around and keep the spacing no more than 1" (2.5cm) apart. You can also do pebbles, loops, leaves or a dogwood shape to list a few. For the dogwood shape I like to draw a grid and the design out with a water-soluble marker and then free motion the design.

Hand Quilting

One of the most beautiful types of quilting is done by hand. It may take longer but in my opinion it is always worth it! In the book, I use three strands of embroidery floss, and use a running stitch to go around a perimeter or highlight a section. This makes the area really pop.

Straight Line Quilting

Stitch vertical and or horizontal lines with your walking foot or many times I use my ¼" (6mm) foot. You can use a quilting bar attachment if you'd like to have the lines perfectly spaced. Drawing lines or grids using a ruler with a water-soluble pen also works great.

Long-arm Quilting

I've always admired the beautiful designs and patterns long-arm quilters can do. They give the quilt a lovely professional finished touch! If you decide to have a long-arm quilter (page 144) do your quilt you can skip the quilt sandwich part. You send your 3 layers to the long-arm quilter and they put it on the long arm machine and quilt the design of your choice. Whether it be flowers, clamshells, waves or a wood grain, you have many options to choose from.

Binding

Binding is the last step in many of the projects in this book. When making a pillow, quilt, pot holder or needlebook you always want to square up your project so the backing, batting, and front is the same size. This will give a nice straight finish to your project. When I bind a project I always make my own binding, the single fold method with mitered corners. I cut 2 ¼" (5.7cm) strips from coordinating fabric. I cut mine cross-wise to save on fabric, but if you prefer you can cut on the bias so it stretches easier. The binding strips should be the sum of all four sides plus 8-10" (20.3-25.4cm).

1 If one strip isn't long enough like in most my projects, join several strips together. To do this, place two strips together at a right angle, right sides facing and draw a diagonal line. Sew on the line, and then cut a ¼" (6mm) away from the line and press the seam open. Repeat until length is long enough for your project.

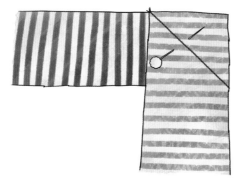

2 Fold the binding strip in half lengthwise and press the raw edges so they are aligned.

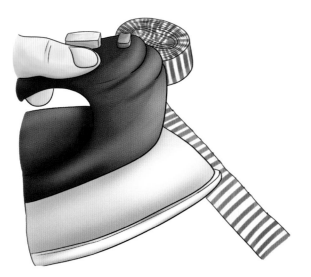

3 Take an end and cut a right angle and then fold the right angle raw edge down a ¼" (6mm). Press the seam again, and then cut off the little dog ear.

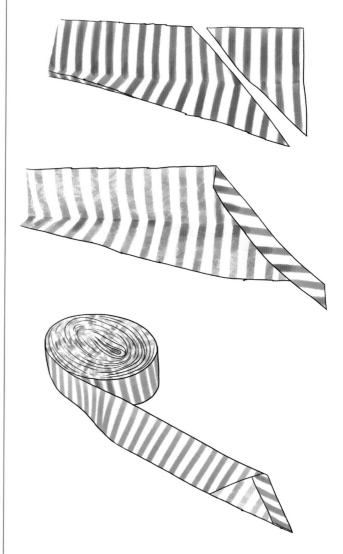

4 Align the raw edge of the binding with the raw edge of the back of the quilt; starting with the end you cut the right angle.

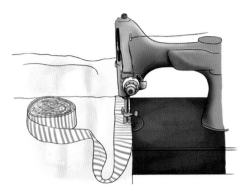

5 Sew a ¼" (6mm) along the edge of the quilt. When you get to the corner pull the quilt out a little and fold the binding up at a right angle and then fold it back down. The raw edges should be even with the edge of the quilt.

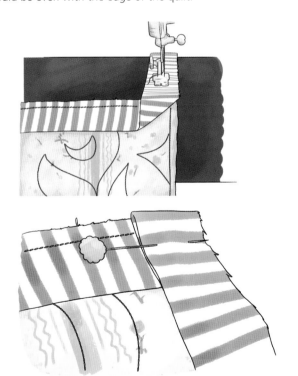

6 Continue sewing a ¼" (6mm) around the quilt and then repeat step 5 at corners.

7 Right before you reach the end, trim any excess binding and then tuck the raw edge into the right angle end you started with.

8 Fold the binding strip over to the front of the quilt. Sew as close the edge as you can.

When you get to the corner, fold the corner down and then back up to make a mitered looking corner and then continue stitching.

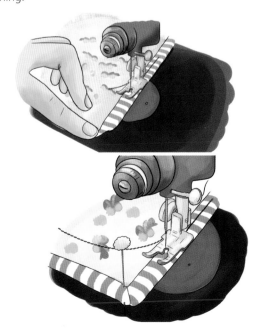

Hand Stitches

Running Stitch

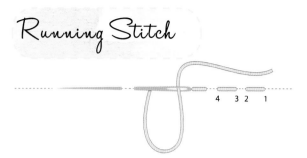

Uses: Outlining, straight and curved lines.

Work from right to left.

Bring thread up at 1 then down at 2, up at 3 and down at 4 and continue. The spaces between the stitches can be the same length as the stitches or shorter for a different look.

TIPS
Keep an even tension and avoid pulling thread or the stitches will pucker.

Back Stitch

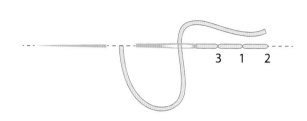

Uses: Outlining, straight and curved lines.

Work from right to left.
Bring needle up at 1 and back down at 2.
Move left and bring needle up at 3, then back down at 1.
Continue stitching.

TIPS
Make shorter stitches for curved lines and shapes.

Whip Stitch

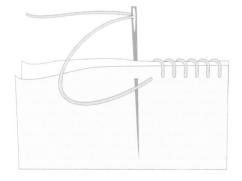

The whipstitch is probably the fastest and easiest stitch to use when hand sewing. It's a good all-purpose stitch and works well for most puppet building fabrics (ie. various fleeces and fur).

With the right sides of the fabric together, push your threaded needle into the wrong side of one of the pieces of fabric, through the second piece of fabric, so that it comes out the wrong side of the second piece. Loop the needle around over the top of where the two pieces come together and again push the needle into the wrong side of the first piece of fabric, through the second, and out. Continue to stitch in this manner for the length of the seam.

Slip Stitch

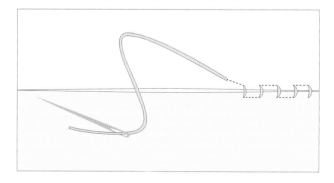

An invisible stitch used to sew two folded edges together. Moving from right to left, take a small stitch out of one side of the folded edge, then move forward and take a small stitch out of the other side. Every so often, pull the thread taut, so that the fabric edges close and the stitches vanish.

Cross Stitch

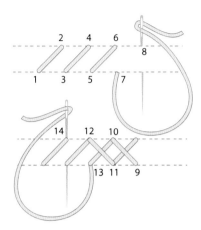

Uses: Borders and filling if worked in adjacent rows.

To stitch a line: Stitching from left to right, bring needle up at 1, down at 2, then up at 3 and down at 4. Continue stitching across to end of line.
Start back stitching from right to left, make crosses by bringing the needle up at 9 and down at 10. Continue until all crosses have been stitched.

TIPS
Be sure to keep the top stitch on the cross the same direction throughout a project.

Straight Stitch

To work this simple stitch bring your needle up at 1 and down at 2 to complete the stitch.

Satin Stitch

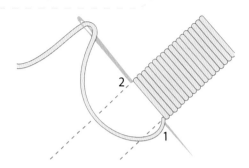

Uses: Solid filling for shapes, great for monograms

Bring needle up at 1, down at 2, then back up right next to 1 and down right next to 2. Place stitches closely together to fill in area. Be sure the thread lays flat and without any twisting to produce a smooth look.

TIPS
To raise the stitching, Split Stitch just inside the outline of the shape before starting.

French Knot

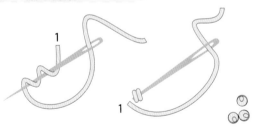

Uses: Decorative dots, filling flower centers, leaves, plants, eyes.

Bring needle up at 1.
Hold thread taut with other hand and wrap the thread twice around end of the needle.
Gently pull the thread so that the wrapped threads tighten and while holding it taut, insert the needle next to 1. Pull thread through onto the backside until the knot is formed and lies securely on the surface.

TIPS
To make a larger knot, wrap the thread around the needle a couple of extra times or use a thicker thread.

Vintage Planter Pincushion

Many years ago I found my first vintage planter while thrift shopping. It was a sweet deer pulling a cart, and it instantly had my heart! After I got it home and placed it on my desk next to a pincushion, I immediately placed the pincushion inside the planter as it was a perfect fit! Now every time I'm thrift shopping I search for these adorable 50's nursery planters. Even my mom, aunts, and friends search for them, so I've gained quite the collection over the years!

You will need

* One vintage planter
* Two rectangles/squares (depends on your planter shape) of low volume fabric
* Seven paper hexagon templates
* Seven fabric scraps for hexagons
* Fusible web
* Polyester fiber-fil
* Hot glue gun with glue
* Contrasting and coordinating thread
* Hand sewing needle
* Scissors

INSTRUCTIONS

1   Measure your planter opening. Depending on the size of the opening print on cardstock and cut out seven ¼" (6mm), 3/8" (1cm), or ½" (1.3cm) hexagons. Or you can purchase the pre-cut hexagons.

2   Make your grandmothers flower garden as instructed in the techniques section under English Paper Piecing (page 12).

3   Measure the opening of your planter. Cut your low volume rectangle/square fabric 2 ½" (6.4 cm) larger. If your planter opening is approx. 3" x 4" (7.6 x 10.2cm) then cut your rectangle to 5 ½" x 6 ½" (14 x 16.5cm). It is alright to use approximate measurements as the planters aren't always perfect rectangles or squares. Though, it is best to round up than round down.

4   Cut a piece of fusible web a little smaller than your flower and place on the back side of the flower. Center the flower on the front side of one of your rectangle/square fabric pieces. Then iron in place.

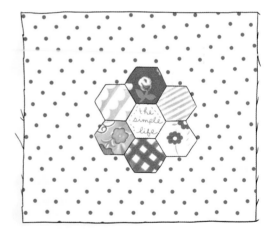

5 Machine appliqué using a short straight stitch around the perimeter of the flower as close to the edge as you can.

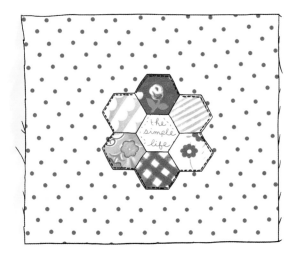

6 Pin your front and back rectangle pieces rights sides together and pin. Sew around all four edges and leave a 2″ (5.1cm) opening for turning. Turn right side out and push out the corners with a turner (a chop stitch can work well).

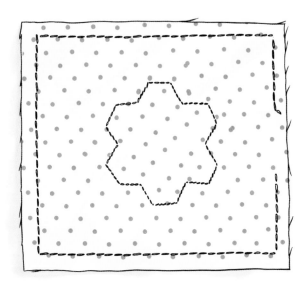

7 Stuff the pincushion with fiber-fil until full. To close the opening, use a slipstitch.

8 Place some fiber-fil in the bottom of the planter opening. Then place the pincushion inside. You may need to work it in from one side to the next. It should fit snug.

9 Use small amounts of hot glue around the inside edges in several places to attach it securely to the planter.

Cozy Cottage Sewing Machine Cover

I love anything handmade in a cottage shape! This sweet cottage sewing machine cover will add the perfect cuteness to your sewing machine while keeping the dust bunnies away!

You will need

* Two, 8 ¾" x 18 ½" (22.2 x 47cm) rectangles, pink floral print, for house
* Two, 5 ¼" x 18 ½" (13.3 x 47cm) rectangle, mint stripe print, for roof
* One, scallop white lace 18 ½" (47cm) long
* One, thick red lace 3" (7.6cm) long
* One, 20" x 28" (50.8 x 71.1cm) rectangle, light pink solid, for backing
* One, 20" x 28" (50.8 x 71.1cm) rectangle, cotton batting
* Four, 1 ½" x 15" (3.8 x 38.1cm) strips, red polka dot print, for ribbon ties
* Four, 2 ¾" x 3 ¼" (7 x 8.3cm) white solid, for windows
* Four, 4" (10.2cm) long, white mini pom pom trim, for windows
* Eight, 2 ¼" x 3" (5.7 x 7.6cm) rectangles, small red gingham print, for window curtains
* Four, 3/8" x 4 ¼" (1 x 10.8cm) diagonal stripe print, for window rods
* One, 3 ½" x 5" (8.9 x 12.7cm) aqua polka dot print, for door
* Three pink scraps pieces for flower on roof
* Cozy cottage templates
* Two buttons, one pink and one red
* Cute fussy cut fabric images for added touches to windows, door and house (optional)
* Fusible web

INSTRUCTIONS

1 Copy roof template onto cardstock and cut out. Take your mint stripe print and place the pattern over it and then trim the two top corners. Do the same with your second mint stripe piece.

2 Machine baste your white scallop lace onto the top edge of your pink floral print.

3 Sew the bottom of your roof piece to the top of your house piece. Do the same with your second roof and house piece and then set that one aside.

4 Print your curtain, door, and flower templates onto cardstock.

5 Trace your curtain template eight times onto a fusible web sheet. Then place your fusible web onto the wrong side of the red gingham print and cut out the curtain shape. Do the same to make your door and flower pieces. Back your cute fussy cut images, windows, and curtain rod strips, and flowers with fusible web too.

6 Center your door and remove the fusible web backing to put in place on the front house piece.

7 Measure and place your white window pieces so they are even. Place your cute fussy cut pieces on windows and then the red gingham curtains. Then, place your curtain rod on the top of the curtains.

8 Center the large flower piece on the roof. Set the medium and small one aside. Press your pieces in place.

9 Fold your red lace in half; pin and machine baste the raw edges to top of the roof.

10 Sew your front house piece to the back house piece.

11 Spray baste your house piece to the batting piece.

12 Machine appliqué with dark thread around your window curtains, rods, fussy cut images, and door. Sew around each piece twice so it really stands out. Machine appliqué your large flower, and then add the medium flower, and then the small flower after each previous piece has been sewn.

13 Sew your white mini pompom pieces onto the bottom of the windows.

14 Hand sew your buttons onto the door and flower.

15 Trim your excess batting around the house.

16 Press your red polka dot strips in half lengthwise and then open back up. Fold both the edges to the center pressed line and fold the top edge down ¼" (6mm) and re-press. Sew along the edge. Repeat to make the other three ribbon ties.

17 Pin your red polka dot ribbon ties in place on the house with raw edges lining up.

18 Place your house piece right sides together with your pink solid piece and pin generously. Sew around all the edges but leave a 2" (5.1cm) opening for turning.

19 Trim your excess pink solid.

20 Turn your house right side out. Use a turner for the corners and then press. Top stitch around all the edges.

Finished Size
18" x 25 ½" (45.7 x 64.8cm)

Heart Coaster

This project is the prefect one to make when you want something cute, simple and quick! To make this you will be using strips instead of tiny little squares so it makes it much easier! Then adding the ric rac gives it the cuteness factor so it brings that special touch to any room!

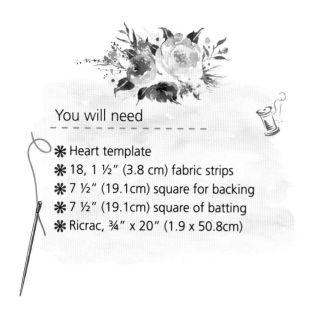

You will need

* Heart template
* 18, 1 ½" (3.8 cm) fabric strips
* 7 ½" (19.1cm) square for backing
* 7 ½" (19.1cm) square of batting
* Ricrac, ¾" x 20" (1.9 x 50.8cm)

INSTRUCTIONS

1 Sew 6, 1 ½" (3.8cm) strips together lengthwise. Make two more sets of 6, 1 ½" (3.8cm) strips so you have a total of 3 sets.

2 Press your seams so they are going in opposite directions.

3 Cut each set with a rotary cutter into two, 1 ½" (3.8cm) patchwork strips. Repeat with your other two sets so you have a total of 6 patchwork 1 ½" (3.8cm) strips.

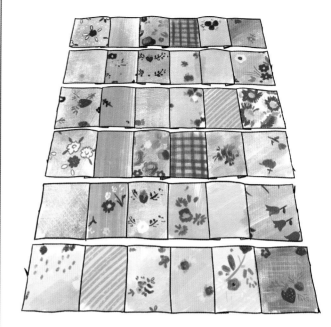

4 Take one strip from each set (set the other three aside) and place the top and bottom right sides together with raw edges matching. Sew along the edge so it is in a loop.

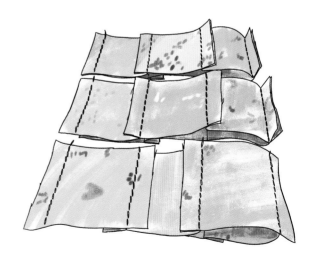

5 Take the bottom seam from the loop and seam rip the seam open so now it's a flat strip again. This makes the arrangements of the patches different from the other three you set aside.

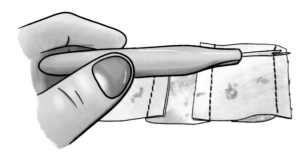

6 Sew the 6 patchwork strips together lengthwise. Press seams open this time. The seams should rest inside each other as you sew them since you pressed them in opposite directions.

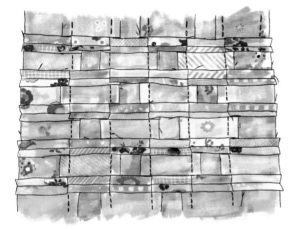

7 Spray baste your patchwork top to your batting and quilt the top.

8 Print your heart template out on cardstock and cut out. Trace your template on the patchwork square and then cut out the heart shape. Repeat with your backing piece.

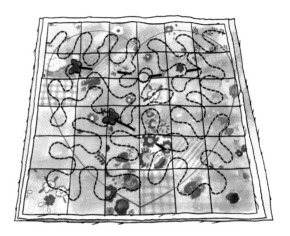

9 Machine baste your ricrac around the top edge of your heart.

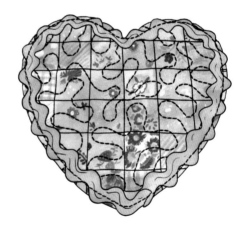

10 Place your patchwork heart and the backing heart right sides together and sew around the outside edge. Leave a 2″ (5.1cm) opening for turning right side out.

11 Turn your heart coaster right side out and then topstitch ⅛″ (3mm) from the edge around your heart.

12 Repeat to make three more coasters so you have a full set.

Ice Skating Girl Pillow

This project takes me back to when my sweet
girls took ice skating lessons. I loved watching
them on the ice. The embroidery was inspired by
a cute vintage 50's Valentine's Day card. I've been
collecting them for years, and love all the sweet
images!

You will need

✳ Four, 3 ½" (8.9cm) squares, low volume cotton print, background

✳ Eight, 4 ½" (11.4cm) squares, grey cotton print, HST

✳ Six, 4 ½" (11.4cm) squares, red cotton print, HST

✳ Six, 4 ½" (11.4cm) squares, aqua cotton print, HST

✳ Four, 4 ½" (11.4cm) squares, pink cotton print, HST

✳ Two, 5 ½" (14cm) squares, grey cotton print, HST

✳ Two 5 ½" (14cm) squares, red cotton print, HST

✳ One, 6 ½" (16.5cm) square, white solid, for background of embroidery

✳ One, 21" x 21" (53.3 x 53.3cm) square cotton print, front-back piece

✳ One, 20" x 20" (50.8 x 50.8cm) square, cotton batting

✳ One, 11 ¾" x 18 ½" (29.8 x 47cm) rectangle cotton print, envelope backing

✳ One, 13 ½" x 18 ½" (34.3 x 47cm) rectangle cotton print, envelope backing

✳ Pre-made double fold binding or 2 ¼" (5.7cm) strip at least 82" (208.2cm) long of cotton print fabric

✳ Basting spray

✳ 8" (20.3cm) embroidery hoop

✳ Water-soluble pen

✳ Ice skating girl embroidery pattern

DMC Floss

✳ Red – 321

✳ Dark Mint – 993

✳ Light Mint – 964

✳ White – Blanc

✳ Pink – 605

✳ Grey – 169

✳ Brown – 898

✳ Cream – 746

Instructions

1 Print the ice skating girl pattern on printer paper and tape to a window. Center the 6 ½" (16.5cm) square over the pattern and tape in place. Trace the pattern with a water-soluble pen. Set aside.

2 To create a HST (half square triangle), take one red 5 ½" (14 cm) square. On the wrong side of the fabric draw a diagonal line from one corner to the opposite corner. Place a grey 5 ½" (14cm) square right sides together with the red square that has the drawn diagonal line. Machine stitch a ¼" (6mm) away from your drawn line on both sides. Cut on the drawn line to make two triangles. Press seams open and trim to 4 ½" (11.4cm).

3 You have two red/grey HST's. Repeat with the other 5 ½" (14cm) red and grey squares so you have 4 red/grey HST's. Draw a diagonal line on the wrong side of the red/grey HST's. Place the four pink 4 ½" squares on the 4 red/grey HST's right sides together. Sew ¼" away from the drawn lines on both sides. Cut on the lines, and then press seams open. Trim to 3 ½" (8.9cm) square. Continue until you have eight, pink/red/grey squares. Set aside.

4 Using the 4 ½" (11.4cm) squares and the instructions in step 2, make eight red/low volume HST's, four red/aqua HST's, and eight aqua/low volume HST's and then trim to 3 ½" (8.9cm) square.

5 Arrange your blocks so the 6 ½" (16.5cm) square is in the middle and then layout the HST's and the 3 ½" (8.9cm) low volume squares so it is in the double star pattern.

6 Using a ¼" (6mm) seam, sew blocks (a, b, c, d, e, f) together starting with the first two with right sides together and then going to the next so you have a row. Continue to the next row and sew blocks (g, h, i, j, k, l). Press seams open. Sew these two rows together and press seam open. Sew blocks, (m,n) together, and (o,p) together and press seams open. Sew these small rows together. Do the same with blocks, (r, s, t, u). Then sew those blocks to the (q) block and press seams open. Continue with (v, w, x, y ,z, 1), sewing these into a row, and (2, 3, 4, 5, 6, 7) into a row. Press seams open and then sew these two rows together.

a	b	c	d	e	f
g	h	i	j	k	l
m	n	q		r	s
o	p			t	u
v	w	x	y	z	1
2	3	4	5	6	7

7 Sew the 3 row sections together so you have an 18 ½" x 18 ½" (47 x 47cm) winter star block.

8 Center the ice skating girl block in the middle of the embroidery hoop. Use 3 strands of embroidery floss for the stitches unless other wise noted.

9 Use a backstitch (embroidery stitches are shown in the technique section) for outlining the dress (dark mint), leggings (dark mint), skates (red), gloves (red), skate blades (grey), hat (red), hair (brown), facial features (using 2 strands of embroidery floss…brown, pink, cream), and ice (light mint).

10 Use a straight stitch to embroider the dress skirt (white) cuffs (white), hat pompom (white), fur socks (white), and snowflakes (light mint).

11 Use a satin stitch to fill in the dress (dark mint), leggings (dark mint), skates (red), gloves (red), and hat (red).

Completing the Pillow

12 Make a quilt sandwich with your pillow top. Take your 18 ½" (47cm) "Ice Skating Girl" winter star block and spray baste your batting piece, and then your 18 ½" (47cm) front-back piece. Hand or machine quilt. I machine stitched around the star part and then hand quilted using a running stitch around the outside of the embroidery.

13 To make your envelope backing, fold and press the top edge of your 11 ¾" x 18" (29.8 x 47cm) cotton print a ¼" (6mm), then fold it again a ¼" (6mm) to make a French seam. Stitch two rows, one an ⅛" (3mm) from the edge and another one a ¼" (6mm) from that line. Do the same with your 13 ½" X 18 ½" (34.3 x 47cm) piece but to the bottom edge.

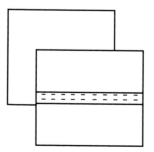

14 Place your pillow top and your envelope backing pieces wrong sides together so they over lap and pin securely. Machine baste around the edges an ⅛" (3mm) to secure the front and envelope backing.

15 Bind the pillow: Use pre-made double fold binding or make your own. To make your own, attach 2 ¼" (5.7cm) strips of a coordinating cotton print until you have approximately 82" (208.2cm) of binding. Press the strips in half lengthwise with right side facing out and raw edges lining up. Bind the quilt using your preferred method. I machine stitch my binding to the back and then turn the binding to the front and machine stitch it in place.

Pretty Pinwheels on Point Quilt

I've always adored classic pinwheel quilts. With this quilt we take the classic pinwheel and set it on point. Then you add some corner stones and borders, and you have a fun and easy variation to the much loved pinwheel quilt.

You will need

* Twelve, 6" (15.2cm) squares, low volume polka dot print, pinwheels
* Twelve, 6" (15.2cm) squares, of a variety of cotton prints, pinwheels
* Two matching 6" (15.2cm) squares, 12 variety cotton prints, (24 total squares), background of pinwheels
* Twenty, 2" (5.1cm) squares, cotton prints in a variety of colors, corner stones
* Thirty one, 2" x 9" (5.1 x 22.9cm) rectangles, low volume polka dot print, sashing
* Two, 2" x 42" (5.1 x 106.7cm) strips, pink cotton print, for inside, side borders
* Two, 2" x 35" (5.1 x 88.9cm) strips, pink cotton print, for inside, bottom and top border
* Two, 3" x 45" (7.6 x 114.3cm) strips, white cotton print, for middle, side borders
* Two, 3" x 40" (7.6 x 101.6cm) strips, white cotton print, for middle, bottom and top border
* Two, 4" x 50" (10.2 x 127cm) strips, aqua cotton print, for outside, side borders
* Two, 4" x 47" (10.2 x 119.4cm) strips, aqua cotton print, for outside, bottom and top borders
* One, approximately 52" x 62" (132.1 x 157.5cm) rectangle of cotton batting
* One, approximately 54" x 64" (137.2 x 162.6cm) rectangle, cotton print or vintage sheet for backing
* Double fold binding or at least 215" (546.1cm) of 2 ¼" (5.7cm) strips of cotton print to make your own binding

INSTRUCTIONS

1 Place one of the 6″ (15.2cm) low volume polka dot squares right sides together with one of the 6″ (15.2cm) cotton print squares. Machine stitch a ¼″ (6mm) around all four outside edges. Rotary cut a diagonal line from the top left corner down to the bottom right corner. Cut another diagonal line from the top right corner down to the bottom left corner. Now you have 4 HST's (half square triangles). Press and trim your HST's to 3 ½″ (8.9cm).

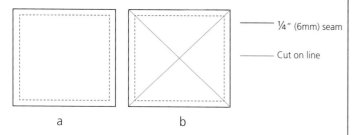

—— ¼″ (6mm) seam

—— Cut on line

a   b

2 Arrange your HST's to make a pinwheel. Machine stitch your pinwheel block together using a ¼″ (6mm) seam.

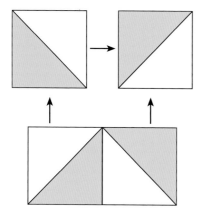

3 Take two of your matching 6″ (15.2cm) squares and cut both of them in half diagonally. Place your long side of the triangle rights sides together with the top of the pinwheel and machine stitch ¼″ (6mm) seam along the top raw edge. Do the same with the bottom edge. Trim the 4 sides then press seams open. Take your other two triangles and machine stitch a ¼″ (6mm) right sides together on the left and right sides of your pinwheel block. Press you seams open, and trim ¼″ (6mm) away from each point. Your block should be 9″ (22.8cm) square.

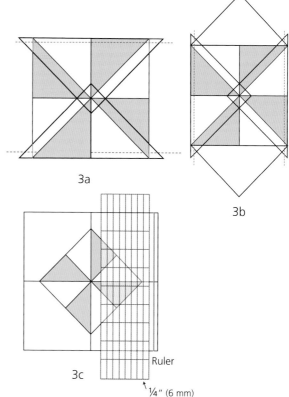

3a

3b

3c   Ruler

¼″ (6 mm)

4 Repeat steps 1 through stop 3 until your have 12 pinwheels on points completed.

5 Arrange the 12 blocks in a pleasing arrangement so the colors are balanced. Lay out the sashing and corner stone pieces. Machine stitch the blocks to the sashing pieces and the sashing and corner stone pieces to make rows.

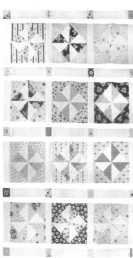

6 Machine stitch your rows together.

7 Next, machine stitch the inside border pieces. Press seams open. Repeat with your top and bottom border pieces. Do the same with your middle and outside border pieces until you have your quilt top completed.

8 Make a quilt sandwich. Lay out the batting piece. Spray the batting piece with basting spray and then lay your quilt top over the batting piece and hand press so it lays flat. Turn your quilt top and batting over so your batting is facing up and spray your batting with basting spray and then lay your backing piece over the batting and hand press so it lays flat.

9 Hand or machine quilt. I had mine long arm quilted so I was able to skip step 8 and sent the quilt sandwich pieces to her (page 144). After it is quilted, trim around the edges of your quilt since the batting and backing pieces are larger.

10 Bind your quilt: Use pre-made double fold binding or make your own. To make your own, attach 2 ¼" (5.7cm) strips of a coordinating cotton print until you have approximately 215" (546.1cm) of binding. Press the strips in half lengthwise with right side facing out and raw edges lining up. Bind the quilt using your preferred method. I machine stitch my binding to the back and then turn the binding to the front and machine stitch it in place.

Spring Flowers Table Runner

In this project we use a classic tulip and daffodil block to create a lovely patchwork table runner. Tulips and daffodils are my favorite flowers. Almost yearly I take the family to a tulip festival north of Seattle to enjoy fields of these beautiful flowers.

You will need

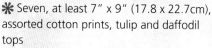

✳ Seven, at least 7" x 9" (17.8 x 22.7cm), assorted cotton prints, tulip and daffodil tops

✳ Seven, at least 3" (7.6cm) squares, assorted cotton prints, tulip and daffodil centers

✳ Seven, fat eighths, assorted low volume prints, background of tulips and daffodils

✳ Seven, 7" x 9" (17.8 x 22.7cm), assorted green cotton prints, tulip and daffodil stems and leaves

✳ Two, 1 ¼" x 8 ½" (3.2 x 21.6cm) strips, low volume cotton dot prints, inside, side borders

✳ Two, 1 ¼" x 29 ½" (4.4cm x 74.9cm) strips, low volume cotton dot prints, inside, top and bottom borders

✳ Sixteen, 2" (5.1cm) squares, assorted cotton prints, patchwork border

✳ Eight, 1 ¾" x 2" (4.4 x 5.1cm) rectangles, assorted cotton prints, patchwork border

✳ Eight, 2" x 6 ¾" (5.1 x 17.1cm) rectangles, assorted cotton prints, patchwork border

✳ Two, 1 ½" x 13" (3.8 x 33cm) strips, low volume cotton dot prints, outside, side borders

✳ Two, 1 ½" x 36" (3.8 x 91.4cm) strips, low volume cotton dot prints, outside, top and bottom borders

✳ One, 18" x 38" (45.7 x 96.5cm) rectangle, cotton batting

✳ One, 19" x 39" (48.3 x 99.1cm) rectangle, cotton print, backing

✳ Double fold binding or at least 110" (279.4cm) of 2 ¼" (5.7cm) strips of cotton print to make your own binding

✳ Tulip, daffodil, and leaf paper piecing patterns

Instructions

1 Copy the tulip, daffodil and leaf templates onto copy paper.

2 Follow the instructions for the method of Foundation Paper Piecing in the Technique section to make your tulip, daffodil and leaf blocks. The finished block should be the same size as the paper template. Make sure to leave the paper attached.

3 Machine stitch your tulip top block to the tulip stem/leaf block with right side facing and sew along the bottom edge of the tulip and top edge of the stem/leaf. Press seams open. Continue stitching your other tulip tops and tulip bottoms and then your daffodil tops and daffodil bottoms so you have seven flower blocks. Keep the paper attached.

4 Place your tulip and daffodil blocks alternating so the colors are in a pleasing arrangement. Machine stitch the first two tulip and daffodil blocks by placing them right sides together and sewing along the long raw edge. Press seams. Continue with the next flower block and so on until you have all your tulips and daffodils stitched together.

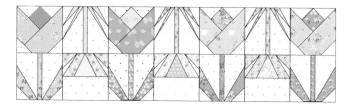

5 Remove your paper from the back of the tulips and daffodils.

6 Attach two strips, one to each side to make your inside border. Press seams. Attach two strips, one to the top and one to the bottom for your inside border. Press seams open.

7 Assemble your two side patchwork borders and press your seams. Attach the side patchwork borders and press seams.

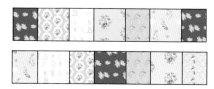

8 Assemble your two top and bottom patchwork borders and press seams. Attach the top and bottom borders and press seams. Next, add the remaining strips to the sides and then the top and bottom to complete the top.

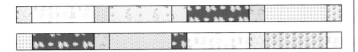

9 Make a quilt sandwich. Lay out the batting piece. Spray the batting piece with basting spray and then lay your table runner top over the batting piece and hand press so it lays flat. Turn your table runner top and batting over so your batting is facing up and spray your batting with basting spray and then lay your backing piece over the batting and hand press so it lays flat.

10 Hand or machine quilt. I free motioned quilted mine with a stippling design by machine.

11 Bind the table runner: Use pre-made double fold binding or make your own. To make your own, attach 2 ¼" (5.7cm) strips of a coordinating cotton print until you have approximately 110" (279.4cm) of binding. Press the strips in half lengthwise with right side facing out and raw edges lining up. Bind the quilt using your preferred method. I machine stitch my binding to the back and then turn the binding to the front and machine stitch it in place.

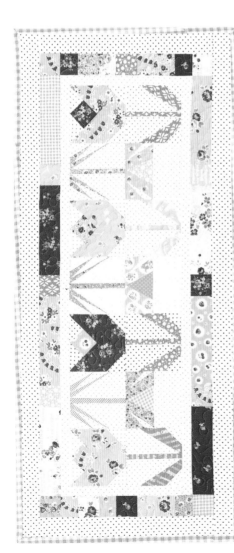

Garden Apron

In the past few years I've really learned to enjoy gardening. Whether it is enjoying the beauty of spring flowers, planting vegetables with the family or working on weeding the flower beds, getting back to the basics is always gratifying. There is something wonderful about spending time in the fresh spring air while making your little garden beautiful! This apron will be the perfect companion as you work!

You will need

Flowers

✳ Twenty eight, 5" (12.5cm) squares in four colors (7 of each color), yo-yo flowers

✳ Clover 1 ¾ inch (45mm) yo-yo maker

✳ Four, ¾" x 7" (1.9 x 17.8cm) long green ricrac for stems

✳ Eight, 2" x 3" (5.1 x 7.6cm) green cotton prints for leaves

✳ Eight, 2" x 3" (5.1 x 7.6cm) green wool felt for leaves

✳ Pinking sheers

✳ Leaf templates

✳ Fusible web

✳ Hand sewing needle

✳ Coordinating thread

Apron

✳ One, 15 ½" x 23" (39.4 x 58.4cm) rectangle, pink floral cotton print, apron front

✳ One, 15 ½" x 23" (39.4 x 58.4cm) rectangle, pink cotton solid, apron back

✳ One, 10" x 23" (25.4 x 58.4cm) rectangle, cotton linen blend, apron pocket

✳ One, 10" x 23" (25.4 x 58.4cm) rectangle pink cotton solid, apron pocket lining

✳ One, 7" x 44" (17.8 x 111.8cm) strip, polka dot cotton print, ruffle

✳ Two, 3 ½" x 42" (8.9 x 106.7cm) strips, gingham cotton print, apron ties

✳ One, 3 ½" x 23 ½" (8.9 x 59.7cm) strip, gingham cotton print, waistband

✳ Water-soluble ink pen

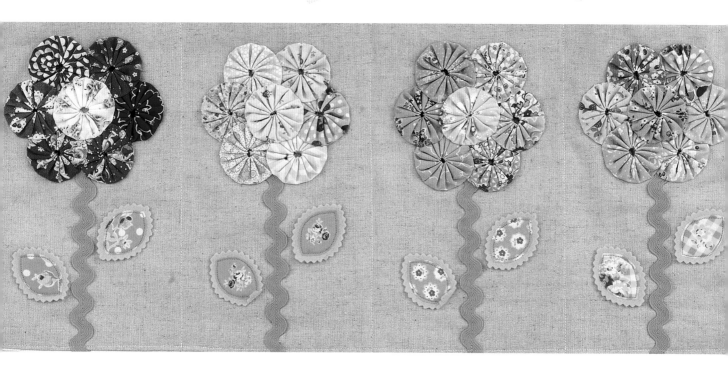

Apron Pocket

1 With your twenty eight, 5" (12.5cm) squares create yo-yo's by following the directions that came with the yo-yo maker.

2 Lay out 6 of the same color yo-yos' in a circular pattern with each one over lapping the next yo-yo. Hand stitch them together where they over lap by using a slip stitch. Place a contrasting yo-yo over the center of your yo-yo circle and attach it to the 6 yo-yos' by using a slip stitch. Continue making 3 more circle yo-yo flowers using the same method.

3 Lay out your linen piece and measure 6" (15.2cm) in and draw a line lengthwise with a water-soluble ink pen. From that line measure 5 ½" (14cm) and draw another line. From that line measure another 5 ½" (14cm) and draw a line. From each raw edge on both sides, measure in a ½" (1.3cm) and draw a line. Center your four green ricrac pieces in each four sections and pin in place. Machine stitch your ricrac in place with coordinating thread by stitching down the center of the ricrac.

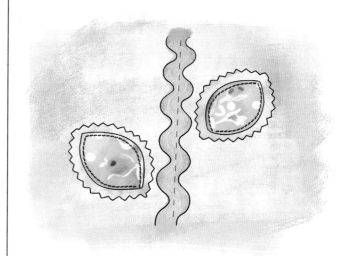

6 Cut a piece of fusible web smaller than each yo-yo flower and place on the backside of each flower. Center each yo-yo flower in a section of the pocket. Iron in place by ironing on the backside of the pocket. Hand stitch each flower to the linen pocket by using a slip stitch.

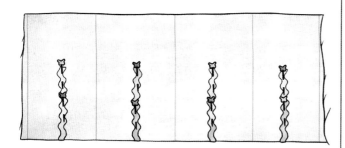

4 Align the pocket lining and the linen pocket right sides together and machine stitch a ½" (1.3cm) along the top and bottom edges (leaving side edges open). Turn right side out and press. Don't use steam or spray water as it will remove your lines.

5 Trace your small and large leaf templates 8 times on fusible web. Cut around the fusible web of each leaf and place the fusible web on the backside of the green cotton print rectangles and cut out. Do the same with the green felt but cut out with pinking sheers. Iron the leaves in place and machine stitch around the outside of the cotton print leaf part to secure them to the pocket.

Apron Skirt

8 Fold the polka dot strip right sides together lengthwise and press. Machine stitch a ¼" (6mm) on the short ends. Turn right side out. Machine baste (a large stitch length), along the top raw edge. Gather the strip by pulling the threads. Gather until the strip is 22 ½" (57.2cm).

7 Place the linen flower pocket on top of the pink floral apron front piece 2" (5.1cm) from the bottom edge of the front piece. Machine Stitch ⅛" (3mm) from the edges along the edges and bottom.

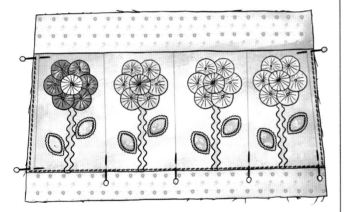

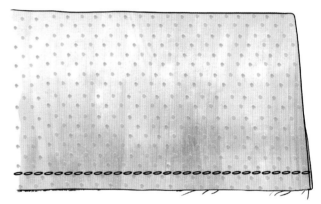

9 Pin the gathered ruffle strip along the bottom raw edge of the apron front. The ruffle should start and stop a ½" (1.3cm) from each end. Top stitch the ruffle in place ¼" (6mm) from the raw edge.

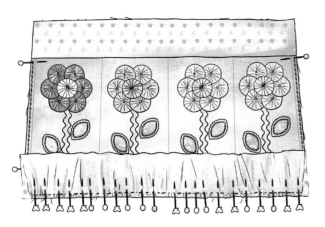

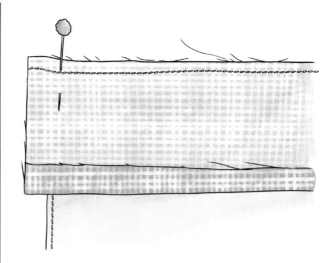

10 Place the apron front right sides together with the solid pink apron back piece. Machine stitch a ½" (1.3cm) along the side and bottom edges. Make sure the ruffle doesn't get caught in the seam. Turn right side out and press.

11 Top stitch along the 3 drawn invisible pen lines to create the pockets. Backstitch several times at the top to make sure it is secure.

12 Take the waistband strip and fold under a ½" (1.3cm) along the long edge, and press. Turn the apron over to the back side and align the waistband strips raw edge along the top edge of the apron. The strip will go over a ½" (1.3cm) on both ends. Pin in place and machine stitch a ¼" (6mm) from the top edge.

13 Press the waistband seam up over the top of the apron. Turn the apron over so the front side is facing up. Press the waistband edges a ½" (1.3cm) in towards the apron.

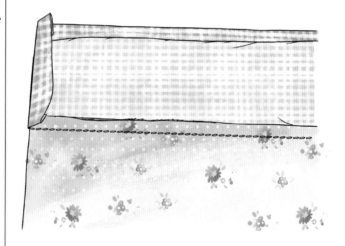

14 Turn apron back over to backside. Fold the top of the waistband down over the edge of the apron and place the apron tie ends inside the waistband and pin in place. Machine stitch a ½" (1.3cm) from the edge.

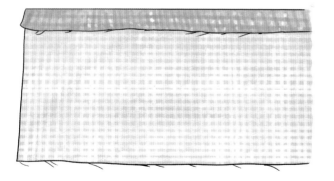

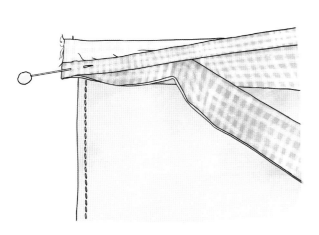

15 Turn the apron back to the front side. Fold the waist-band to the front so it is right side out. Align the folded edge to the top of the apron along the seam and pin in place. Top stitch the waistband close to the edge and stitch around the entire waistband and apron ties. Spray water on the water-soluble ink marks so they disappear.

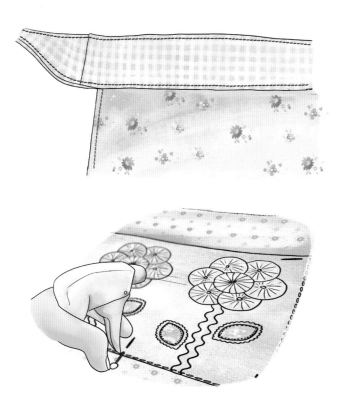

Cross Stitch Sewing Book

When I go to parks, beaches, appointments, or on road trips I love to take a hand sewing project along. This project is a lovely sewing book that will help you keep your hand sewing project nice and organized.

You will need

Front Cover Block
* One cross stitch 3 ½" (8.9cm) square on gingham
* Four blue cotton print corner squares, 3 ½" (8.9cm)
* Twelve low volume cotton print squares, 2" (5.1cm)
* Four pink cotton print squares, 2" (5.1cm)
* Four blue cotton print rectangles, 2" x 3 ½" (5.1 x 8.9cm)
* Four pink cotton print rectangles, 2" x 3 ½ " (5.1 x 8.9cm)
* One cotton print square, 9 ½" (24.1cm), back piece
* Two pink gingham rectangles, 2 ½" x 9 ½" (6.4 x 24.1cm), one for outside and one for inside

Inside Pieces
Left side
* One cotton print square, 9 ½" (24.1cm), back piece
* Two cotton print rectangles, 7 ½" x 9 ½" (19.1 x 24.1cm), front and back lining of large pocket
* Two cotton print rectangles, 5 ¼" x 9 ½" (13.3 x 24.1cm), front and back lining of small pocket
* Two, cotton print strips, 2" x 10" (5.1 x 25.4cm), binding for pockets
* One cotton print strip, 1 ½" x 9" (3.8 x 22.9cm), ribbon for thread holder

Right side
* One piece of lace, ½" x 4" (1.3 x 10.2cm)
* One rectangle of pink wool felt, 3" x 8" (7.6 x 20.3), needle book
* One cotton print rectangle, 4" x 4 ½" (10.2 x 11.4cm), left side hexie pocket
* One cotton print rectangle, 4 ½" x 6" (11.4 x 15.2cm), right side pocket
* One cotton print rectangle, 4 ½" x 9 ½" (11.4 x 24.1cm), pocket lining
* One ½" (1.3cm) hexie flower
* One cotton print strip, 2" x 10" (5.1 x 25.4cm), binding for pocket
* Double fold binding or at least 65" (165.1cm) of 2 ¼" (5.7cm) strips of cotton print to make your own binding
* Two cotton print strips, 1 ½" x 12" (3.8 x 30.5cm), ribbon ties
* Velcro rectangle, ¼" x ½" (6mm x 1.3cm)
* One rectangle of cotton batting, approximately 12" x 23" (30.5 x 58.4cm)

DMC Floss
* Dark Pink- 603
* Light Pink- 963
* Red- 304
* Dark Green- 701
* Light Green- 704

INSTRUCTIONS

1 Trace the cross stitch pattern onto the gingham
3 ½" (8.9cm) square.

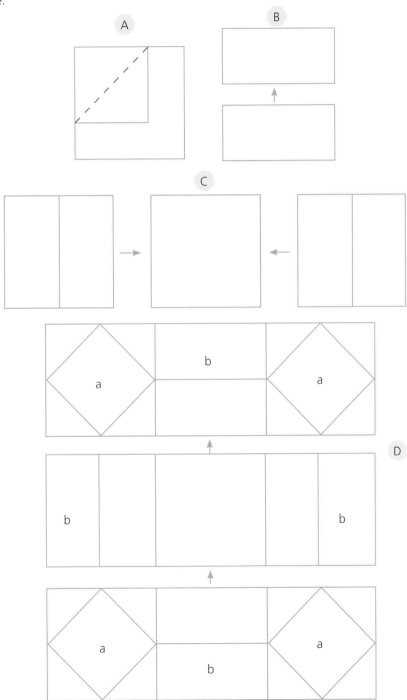

2 **a.** Take 3 low volume 2″ (5.1cm) squares, and 1 pink rose cotton print square the same size and draw a diagonal line down the center from one corner to the opposite corner on the wrong side of the fabric. Take one of your 3 ½″ (8.9cm) cotton print squares and place one, 2″ (5.1cm) square on one of the corners, and another square on the opposite corner and stitch on the line and then rotary cut ¼″ (6mm) away from the line. Press seams open. Repeat this step with the other 2 opposite corners until you have your "a" block complete. Make 3 more "a" blocks as shown in diagram "d".

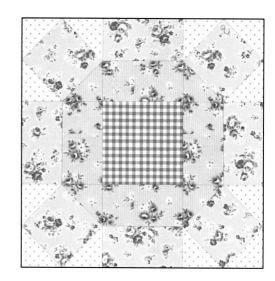

4 Join your 3 front pieces, 9 ½″ (24.1cm) square, cross stitch patchwork square, and one, 2 ½″ x 9 ½″ (6.4 x 24.1cm) gingham rectangle cotton print together using a ¼″ (6mm) seam and press seams open.

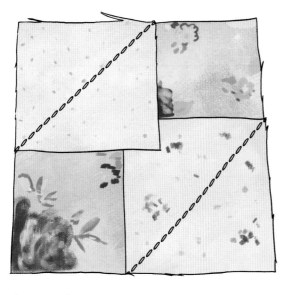

b. Take one pink cotton rectangle, and one aqua cotton print rectangles and place right sides together. Stitch a ¼″ (6mm) seam along one of the long sides and then press seams open. Continue with your other rectangle pieces to create 3 more "b" blocks.

c. Lay out your 9 blocks. Stitch your top 3 blocks together to create a row. Continue and stitch your middle 3 blocks together and then your bottom 3 blocks together so you have 3 rows. Press seams open.

d. Stitch your rows together right sides together and then press seams open.

3 Follow the cross stitch diagram (page 130) and cross stitch the rose. Start with one color and then move onto the different colors when finished with the previous.

5 Spray baste your batting piece to your front cover. Quilt as desired. I machine stitched around the squares and rectangles. Trim the batting and then set the cover aside.

6 Fold your two 2″ x 10″ (5.1 x 25.4cm) binding strip pieces in half lengthwise so raw edges are lined up. Align the small pocket piece, 5 ¼″ x 9 ½″ (13.3 x 24.1cm) with the small pocket lining. Machine stitch the binding on with the raw edges aligned to the top back edge of the pocket lining. Stitch a ¼″ (6mm) seam. Fold the binding over to the front and press. Pin in place along the top edge. Machine stitch as close to the edge of the binding. Repeat with the large pocket.

7 Layout your small pocket on top of the large pocket and then the large pocket on top of one of the 9 ½″ (24.1cm) square cotton prints. Stitch ⅛″ (3mm) around all four edges to secure the pockets in place. Set aside.

8 Create a ½" (1.3cm) grandmothers flower garden by using the English paper piecing method shown in the technique section. Press and remove the basting stitches and take the paper out. Cut a piece of fusible web a little smaller than your flower and place on the backside of the flower. Center the flower on the front side of the 4" x 4 ½" (10.2 x 11.4cm) rectangle cotton print. Iron in place. Machine stitch around the flower as close to the edge as you can.

9 Align the hexagon flower piece and the 4 ½" x 6" (11.4 x 15.2cm) cotton print right sides together. Machine stitch a ¼" (6mm) seam and press seam open. Add the pocket lining and binding strip the same way you did in step 6.

10 Use scallop or pinking sheers to cut a decorative edge around the felt rectangle piece (optional). Fold the felt in half and machine stitch in place with the lace piece, on the 9 ½" x 9 ½" (24.1 x 24.1cm) cotton print. Align the pocket lining along the bottom edge of the 9 ½" (24.1cm) cotton print square. Machine stitch ⅛" (3mm) around the pocket edge to secure in place.

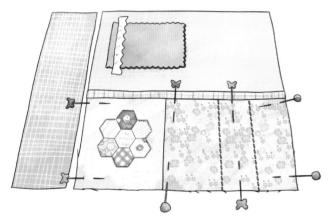

11 Make your ribbon spool holder and your two ties by folding and pressing your cotton print strips in half, open them and fold the raw edges to the folded line and press again. Fold one end in ¼" (6mm) and then machine stitch around both edges of the ribbon close to the edge. Machine stitch one side of the Velcro piece onto the back side of the ribbon spool holder. Machine stitch the other Velcro piece centered and a ½" (1.3cm) from the raw edge of the pink gingham rectangle, 2 ½" x 9 ½" (6.4 x 24.1cm). Machine stitch the top raw edge of the thread holder to the raw edge of the top of the pink gingham rectangle ⅛" (3mm), to secure it in place.

12 Join your 3 lining pieces (2 pocket sides, and gingham rectangle cotton print) together using ¼" (6mm) seam and press seams open.

13 Spray baste the lining to the front cover and machine stitch ⅛" (3mm) around all four sides to secure in place. Machine stitch the ribbon ties in place ⅛" (3mm) from the raw edge.

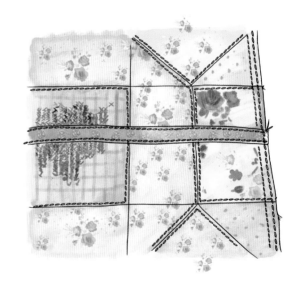

14 Bind the sewing book: Use pre-made double fold binding or make your own. To make your own, attach 2 ¼" (5.7cm) strips of a coordinating cotton print until you have approximately 65" (165.1cm) of binding. Press the strips in half lengthwise with right side facing out and raw edges lining up. Bind the quilt using your preferred method. I machine stitch my binding to the back and then turn the binding to the front and machine stitch it in place.

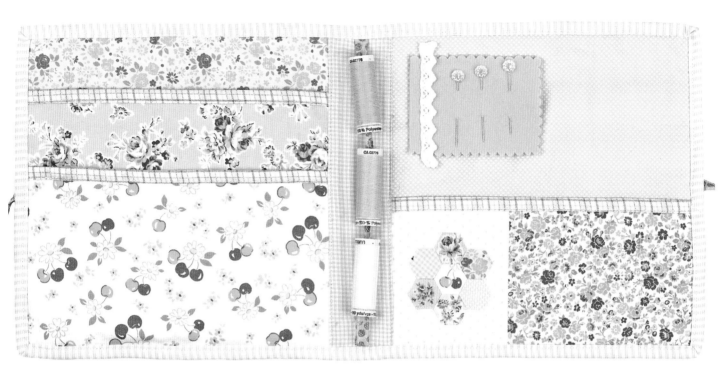

Nautical Sailboat Pillow

Summertime reminds me of warm days on the beach watching the sailboats float by! Taking my family to the beach is one of my favorite things to do. This sailboat pillow reminds me of the many hours we spend on the beach each year.

You will need

* Five, 2 ½" (6.4cm) squares, aqua cotton prints, small sail and boat
* Two, 2 ½" (6.4cm) squares, white cotton solid, small sail and boat
* One, 2 ½" x 4 ½" (6.4 x 11.4cm) rectangle, white cotton solid, background
* One, 1 ½" x 8 ½" (3.8 x 21.6cm) rectangle, white cotton solid, background
* One, 1 ½" x 4 ½" (3.8 x 11.4cm) rectangle, white cotton solid, background
* One, 4 ¼" x 7 ½" (10.8 x 19.1cm) rectangle, white cotton solid, background
* One, 4 ½" (3.8cm) square, navy cotton print, large sail
* One, 4 ½" (3.8cm) square, white cotton solid, large sail
* One, 2 ½ x 8 ½" (6.4 x 21.6cm) rectangle, fish cotton print, water
* One, ¾" x 7 ½" (1.9x 19.1cm) rectangle, red cotton print, pole
* Eight small cotton print scraps for bunting
* 24, 2 ½" (6.4cm) squares, various cotton prints, patchwork border
* One, 14" x 17 ½" (35.7 x 44.5cm) cotton solid, front-back piece
* One, 62" (157.5cm) long pompom trim
* Button
* One, 13 ½" x 17" (34.3 x 43.2cm), cotton batting
* Two, 11 ½" x 13 ½" (29.2 x 34.2cm), cotton print, envelope backing
* Fusible web
* Basting spray

INSTRUCTIONS

1 To create the three small HST's (half square triangles), take three aqua 2 ½" (6.4cm) squares. On the wrong side of the fabric draw a diagonal line from one corner to the opposite corner. Place two of the aqua squares right sides together with the white cotton solid squares. Align the other third aqua square on the left side of the 2 ½" x 4 ½" (6.4 x 10.8cm) rectangle white cotton solid. Machine stitch on the line and then trim a ¼" (6mm) away from your stitched line. Press seams open and cut off the little triangles. Repeat to make the large HST with the 4 ½" (10.8cm) squares.

2 Machine stitch the half square rectangle (a), the large HST (b), and the 1 ½" x 4 ½" (3.8 x 11.4cm) (c). Stitch the red ¾" x 7 ½" (1.9 x 19.1cm) rectangle (d) to the section you just stitched, and then add the 4 ¼" x 7 ½" (3.8 x 19.1cm) rectangle (e).

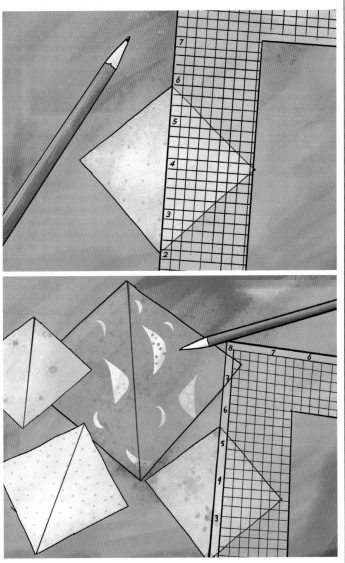

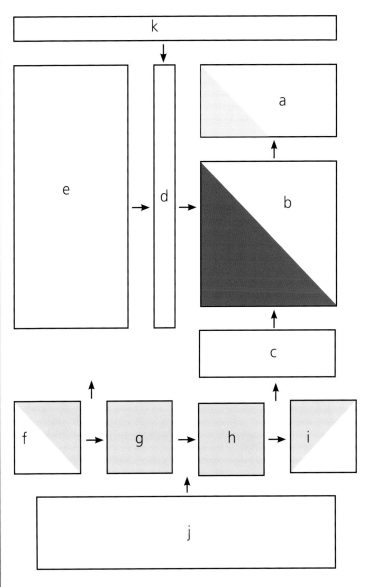

3 Create your boat by machine stitching a 2 ½" (6.4cm) HST (f), 2 ½" (6.4) square (g), 2 ½" (6.4cm) square (h) and the other 2 ½" (6.4cm) HST (i) to create a row. Attach that row to the bottom of the previous section you created in step 2. Add the 2 ½" x 8 ½" (6.4 x 21.6cm) fish print (j) to the bottom of the boat. Lastly, attach the top 1 ½" x 8 ½" (3.8 x 21.6cm) rectangle (k) to the sailboat block.

4 Cut out 8 small triangles from the 8 small cotton print scraps and back with fusible web. Place the eight bunting triangles on the white background section next to the red pole in a manner that is pleasing to the eye. Press in place. Machine stitch with a dark thread around each bunting twice and machine stitch a line that goes from flag to flag to create a bunting.

5 With the 24 patchwork squares, create four, 6 square strips. Machine stitch the first two (a,b) to the left and right sides of the sailboat. Then stitch the other patchwork two strips (c,d) to the top and bottom.

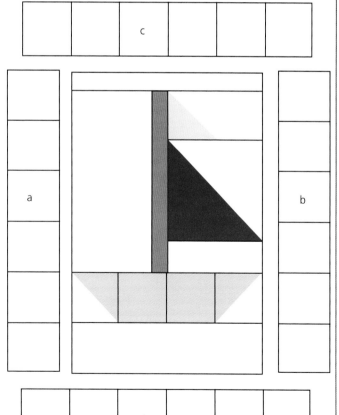

Completing the Pillow

6 Make a quilt sandwich with your pillow top. Spray baste your batting piece, take your 12 ½" x 16 ½" (31.8 x 41.9cm) sailboat block and hand press onto the batting. Turn over and spray baste the other side of batting and hand press the front-back piece to the batting. Hand or machine quilt. I machine free-motion stippled the sailboat block.

7 Hand sew the button in place above the red pole.

8 Machine stitch your pompom trim around all edges of the pillow stitching a ⅛" (3mm) from the edge.

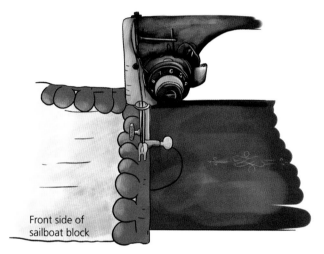

Front side of sailboat block

9 To make your envelope backing, fold and press the top edge of your 11 1/2" X 13 1/2" (29.2 x 32.2cm) cotton print ½" (1.3cm) down. Then fold it again ½" (6mm) to make a French seam. Stitch two rows, one a ⅛" (3mm) from the edge and another one a ¼" (6mm) from that line. Do the same with your second envelope backing piece.

10 Place your pillow top and your envelope backing pieces right sides together and pin liberally to secure in place. Make sure your pompom trim is pinned out of the way. Machine stitch around all edges ¼" (6mm) from the edge. The backing should be larger than the pillow and go over the edges. Let the extra hang over the edges so you have room to work with. After you have stitched around all edges trim the overlap. Since there isn't a binding, secure it again and stitch around the edges a second time or zigzag stitch the edges.

Patchwork Market Tote

Summertime always brings markets! Whether it is a farmers market or a vintage market I love getting out in the fresh air and attending. This tote is the perfect size to bring along so you can fill it with all items you find!

You will need

❋ Eighty Six, 2 ½" (6.4cm) squares, cotton prints, exterior top

❋ One, 12" (30.5cm) square, low volume polka dot, front embroidered piece

❋ Two, 8 ½" x 9" (21.6 x 22.7cm) rectangle, low volume polka dot, front lining, & back lining pocket

❋ Market Day embroidery pattern

❋ 10" (25.4cm) Embroidery Hoop

❋ Water-soluble pen

❋ One, 8 ½" x 9" (21.5 x 22.7cm) rectangle, large fussy cut cotton print, back pocket

❋ Two, 8 ½" x 9" (21.5 x 22.7cm) rectangle, cotton batting, pocket

❋ Two, 8 ½" x 10 ½" (21.5 x 26.7cm) rectangle, aqua gingham, front & back inside pocket

❋ Two, ½" x 9" (1.3 x 22.7cm), elastic lace, pocket trim

❋ Two, 14 ½" x 18 ½" (36.8 x 47cm), cotton batting, top

❋ Two, 5 ½" x 18 ½" (14 x 47cm) rectangle, low volume polka dot, exterior bottom

❋ Two, 5 ½" x 18 ½" (14 x 47cm) cotton batting, bottom

❋ Two, 18 ½" x 19 ½" (47 x 49.5cm), cotton print, lining

❋ Two, 46" (116.8cm) long webbing, straps

DMC Floss
❋ Aqua - 3766
❋ Mint - 959
❋ Red - 321
❋ Yellow - 744
❋ Pink - 605
❋ Navy Blue - 823

*3 strands of embroidery floss are used throughout the embroidery

INSTRUCTIONS

1 Copy the Market Day embroidery pattern onto copy paper. Tape to a window and transfer the pattern with a water-soluble pen onto the 12" (30.5cm) square low volume polka dot print.

2 Outline the following with a backstitch the bird body (mint), feet (yellow), eye (aqua), and beak (yellow). Also outline with a back stitch-- the basket (pink), kerchief (red), market day text (navy blue), market stand (red), market roof (aqua) and bunting (red, mint, pink, and yellow).

3 Using a straight stitch outline the path (red), grass (mint), and birds face (mint).

4 With a satin stitch fill in the eye (aqua), and roof stripes (aqua).

5 Make the polka dots (red) in the kerchief with French knots.

6 Trim the embroidery piece down to 8 ½" x 9" (21.5 x 22.7cm). Set aside.

7 Layout 43, 2 ½" (6.4cm) squares and the gingham 8 ½" x 10 ½" (21.5 x 26.7cm) piece. Start stitching them together in sections until your front top is complete. Repeat so you have the back top piece.

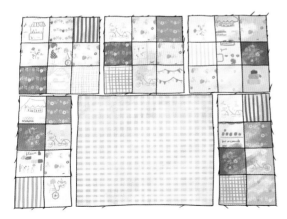

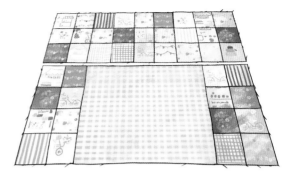

8 Spray baste the front patchwork piece with the front batting piece and machine or hand quilt the squares. Repeat with the back top piece, front and back bottom pieces. For the bottom pieces I measured in 4 ¼" (10.8cm) and 5" (12.7cm) from each side and then drew lines with a water-soluble marker to create an X pattern.

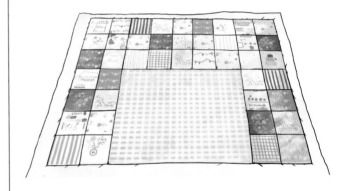

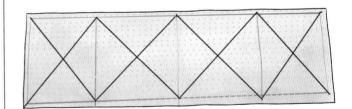

9 Take the embroidered Market Day piece and machine stitch the lace to the top edge. Layer the embroidered piece and a low volume 8 ½" x 9" (21.5 x 22.7cm) piece right sides together and then align the same size cotton batting piece behind the two pieces. Machine stitch a ¼" (6mm) along the top raw edge. Turn, press and then top stitch along the edge. Repeat with your back pocket pieces.

10 Take your front patchwork piece and place the embroidered pocket piece on top and center. Pin in place. Lay out the webbing strap and pin in place overlapping it over the edge of the pocket and lining up with the edge of the patchwork squares. With coordinating thread top stitch the webbing down on both sides of each edge. **STOP at least a ½" (1.3cm) from the top edge on each side.**

11 Place the exterior bottom piece on top the exterior top piece with right sides together. Machine stitch a ¼" (6mm) seam along the bottom edge. Press seams open. Repeat with the back exterior pieces. Align the exterior front and back pieces right sides together and machine stitch a ¼" (6mm) seam along the two sides and the bottom edge.

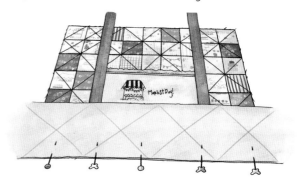

12 Place the lining pieces rights sides together and machine stitch a ¼" (6mm) seam along the sides and bottom. Leave a 4 ½" (11.4cm) opening along the middle bottom edge. Take one corner of the bottom edge and form a triangle and measure 2" (5.1cm) in. Draw a line and sew along the line. Trim ¼" (6mm) from the line. Repeat with the other side. Also, repeat on both bottom corners of the exterior patchwork front/back.

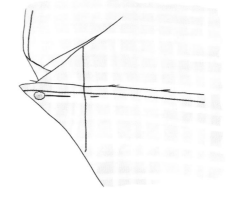

13 Turn the exterior patchwork bag right side out. Place the exterior bag inside the lining. Match the side seams and pin in place. Make sure the straps are tucked inside the bag. Machine stitch ¼″ (6mm) along the top edge all the way around.

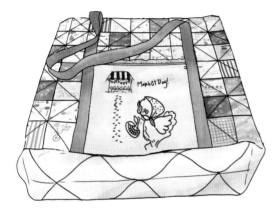

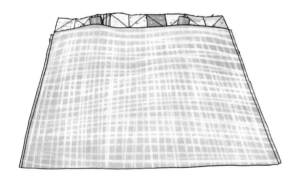

14 Stuff the bag through the 4 ½″ (11.4cm) opening to turn right side out.

15 Close the hole by sewing along the opening. Place the lining inside the bag and press. Topstitch around the top edge as a finishing touch.

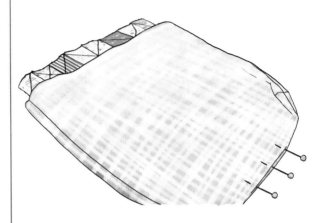

Strawberry Patchwork Bag

This project combines a couple of my favorite things!
Strawberries and patchwork. I simply adore anything strawberry.
Maybe because they are cute and yummy! I find myself leaving out
strawberry things all year long because I love them that much.

You will need

❋ Thirty, 2 ½" (6.4cm) squares, scrappy cotton prints, exterior front

❋ Six, 2 ½" x 3 ½" (6.4 x 8.9cm) rectangles, scrappy cotton prints, exterior front

❋ Strawberry body pattern

❋ Strawberry leaf pattern

❋ One, 13" x 15" (33 x 38.1cm) rectangle, pink strawberry cotton print, exterior back

❋ Three, 13" x 15" (33 x 38.1cm) rectangle, pink cotton solid, lining pieces & back of exterior front

❋ Two, 2 ½" x 12 ½" (6.4 x 31.8cm) rectangles, aqua polka dot print, channels for the loop straps

❋ Four, 4" x 12 ½" (10.2 x 31.8cm) rectangles, aqua polka dot print, leaves

❋ Two, 3" (7.6cm) long ribbon pieces, loops for straps

❋ 4 yards (3.7m), pre-made double fold bias tape or thick cording/string

INSTRUCTIONS

1 Layout the thirty 2 ½" (6.4cm) squares and the six 2 ½" x 3 ½" (6.4 x 8.9cm) rectangles in 7 rows of 6 with the rectangles as the first row. Stitch your squares together into rows. After all the rows are stitched together lay your strawberry body pattern over your patchwork and cut out. Take your back piece and lining pieces and lay the strawberry body pattern on top and cut out. Set aside.

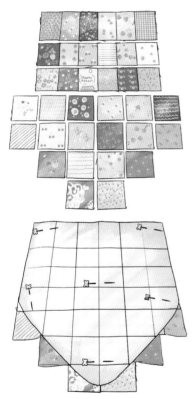

2 Place two of the 4" x 12 ½" (10.2 x 31.8cm) rectangles right sides together and sew a ¼" (6mm) seam along one of the short ends. Lay the rectangle wrong side up and trace the leaf pattern on the wrong side of fabric.

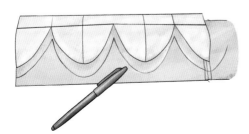

3 Take the two ends of the rectangles and place them right sides together and sew a ¼" (6mm) to make a continuous loop. Repeat with your other two so you have 2 loops (the second loop doesn't need the pattern drawn on). Place the second loop inside the first loop with right sides together and pin at the seams.

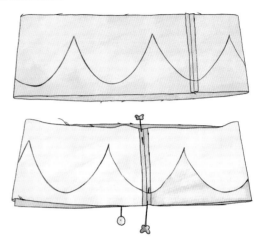

4 Sew along the scallop line all the way around the loop. It may be helpful to shorten your stitch length for this part. Trim away the excess so you have about a ¼" (6mm) around the scallop. Turn right side out. Press, and top stitch around the scallop leaf edge. Set aside.

5 Place the patchwork exterior piece on top of a solid pink strawberry shape piece. Quilt as desired. I did straight line quilting along the seams.

6 For the channels, take an aqua polka dot 2 ½" x 12 ½" (6.4 x 31.8cm) rectangle and fold the ends in a ¼" (6mm), press, and then fold another ¼" (6mm) in and press again. Sew along the seams. Fold in half along the long edge and press. Repeat with the second 2 ½" x 12 ½" (6.4 x 31.8cm) piece.

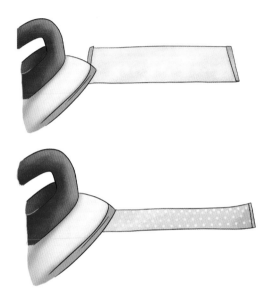

7 Place the channel on the patchwork exterior piece at the top edge with raw edges lining up. The ends should be a ½" (1.3cm) in from the edge on both sides. Topstitch along the fold to secure it to the patchwork exterior piece. Repeat with the second channel piece and the exterior strawberry back piece.

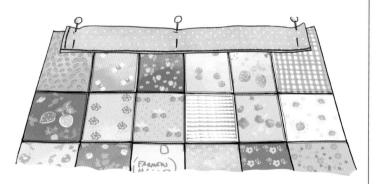

8 Add your strap loops by folding your ribbon in half and placing on top of the patchwork piece with raw edges matching up. Secure the loops to the patchwork piece by stitching ⅛" (3mm) from the edge.

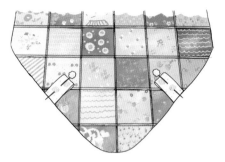

9 Place the exterior patchwork piece right sides together with the exterior back piece and pin in place. Sew a ¼" (6mm) seam along all the sides except the top. Repeat with the two lining pieces but leave an opening along one edge for turning. Set the lining piece aside.

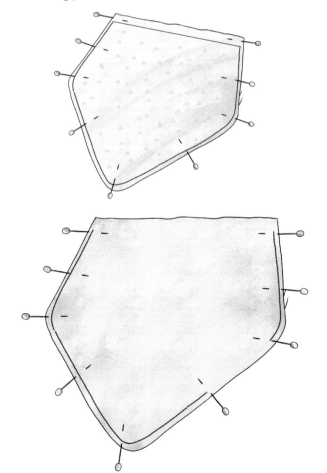

10 Turn the patchwork bag right side out and pin the leaf piece around the top edge with raw edges lining up. Sew a ½" (1.3cm) seam allowance around the top to secure the leaf piece. Place the patchwork bag inside the lining piece and pin along the top raw edges. Sew a ½" (1.3cm) seam allowance along the top edge.

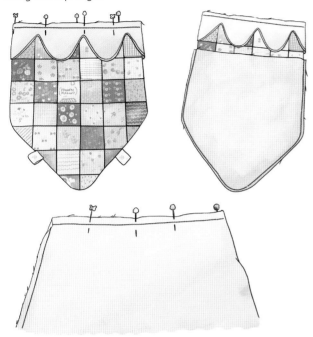

11 Turn the bag right side out through the hole and top stitch the hole closed. Tuck the lining into the bag and press. Topstitch along the top edge.

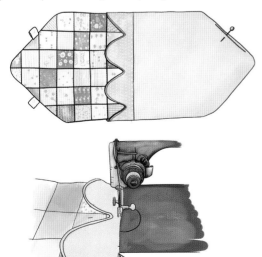

12 For the straps you can use pre-made double fold bias tape (which I used), or thick string like parachute cord (found in jewelry section in the craft store). For double fold bias tape, fold the edges in twice and press, then sew along the open edge. You will need two pieces 46" (116.8cm) for a toddler, 60" (152.4cm) for children, or 70" (177.8cm) for an adult.

13 Attach a safety pin to the end of one of the straps. Feed the strap into the channel opening at the top of the bag. Keep feeding it through until the safety pin reaches the end of the first channel. Pull the safety pin out of the channel and feed it through the other channel so it goes through the other side of the bag. Feed it through till it reaches back to where you started. Repeat with the second strap but start on the other side feeding it the opposite direction.

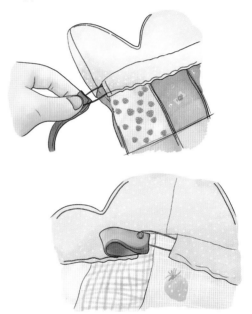

14 Place one strap end through the loop and one end out of the loop. Tie the strap into a knot. You can add a cute charm through the loop for a cute finishing touch.

Cherry Potholder

I love making new kitchen accessories. We spend countless hours in the kitchen preparing yummy food for our family, so why not use cute handmade accessories to brighten that time up?!? This project showcases two red hexagon flowers, a felt stem and leaves which create an adorable cherry!

You will need

* Fourteen red cotton print scraps
* Fourteen, ½" (1.3cm) hexagon templates
* Leaf pattern
* Stem pattern
* Two, green wool felt scraps, leaves
* One, brown wool felt scrap, stem
* Two, green cotton print scraps, leaves
* One, 7" x 7" (17.8 x 17.8cm), linen fabric, background
* Two, 1" x 7" (2.5 x 17.8cm) pink cotton print strips, inside border
* Two, 1" x 8" (2.5 x 20.3cm) pink cotton print strips, inside border
* Two, 1" x 8" (2.5 x 20.3cm) aqua cotton print strips, outside border
* Two, 1" x 9" (2.5 x 22.9cm) aqua cotton print strip, outside border
* Pre-made double fold binding or one 2 ¼"(5.7cm) strip 44"(111.8cm) long of cotton print fabric
* One, 10" x 10" (25.4 x 25.4cm) cotton batting
* One, 10" x 10" (25.4 x 25.4cm) insul-bright (insulated lining)
* One, 10 ½" x 10 ½" (26.7 x 26.7cm) cotton print, backing
* One, 4" (10.2cm) long ribbon or lace, loop
* DMC Floss, aqua - 993 (3 strands)
* Double sided fusible web
* Hand sewing needle
* Pinking or scallop shears

INSTRUCTIONS

1 Print on cardstock and cut out fourteen ½" (1.3cm) hexagons. Or you can purchase the pre-cut hexagons. Make your grandmothers flower garden as instructed in the Techniques section under English Paper Piecing.

2 Print on cardstock and cut out the leaf and stem templates. Follow the instructions in the Technique section for Raw Edge Appliqué to appliqué the stem, and leaves. Use pinking or scallop shears when cutting out the felt leaves and then add another piece of fusible web to the backside of the leaves.

3 Cut two pieces of fusible web a little smaller than your cherry hexagon pieces and place on the backside of the cherries. Arrange the leaves, stem and cherry onto the linen piece.

4 Machine appliqué using a short straight stitch around the perimeter of the cherries, stem and leaves with coordinating thread as close to the edge as you can.

5 Sew the two pink 1" x 7" (2.5 x 17.8cm) strips to the sides of the linen piece and then sew the pink 1" x 8" (2.5 x 20.3cm) strips to the top and bottom. Add the aqua 1" x 8" (2.5 x 20.3cm) strips to the left and right side and then the aqua 1" x 9" (2.5 x 22.9cm) strips to the top and bottom.

6 Layer and spray baste the potholder top to the insul-bright and cotton batting. Hand stitch using a running stitch around the outside of the linen with the aqua DMC floss. Spray baste the backing piece to the batting.

7 Center and pin the ribbon/lace to the back of the potholder with raw edges lining up with the edges at the top of the potholder. Machine baste to secure it using a ⅛" (3mm) seam.

8 Bind the potholder: Use pre-made double fold binding or make your own. To make your own, use a 2 ¼" (5.7cm) strip approximately 44" (111.8cm) long of a coordinating cotton print. Press the strip in half lengthwise with right side facing out and raw edges lining up. Bind the potholder using your preferred method. I machine stitch my binding to the back and then turn the binding to the front and machine stitch it in place.

Lemonade Jug Rug

I love making mug rugs in the winter time! The lemonade jug rug is a perfect version for those hot summer days when we need a refreshing cold drink like lemonade!

You will need

* ✳ Four pink cotton print scraps, roof
* ✳ Four yellow cotton print scraps, roof, lemonade & lemon
* ✳ One red cotton print scrap, lemonade stand poles
* ✳ One, 3" x 6" (7.6 x 15.2cm) pink cotton print, front stand
* ✳ One, 2" x 3 ½" (5.1 x 8.9cm) rectangle, white solid, sign
* ✳ Three, aqua cotton print scraps, pitcher, glass, tape (for sign)
* ✳ One, linen scrap, pitcher handle
* ✳ One, red stripe cotton print scrap, straw
* ✳ One, green cotton print scrap, lemon leaf
* ✳ One, 8" (20.3cm) square, linen
* ✳ Lemonade stand pattern pieces
* ✳ Pre-made double fold binding or one 2 ¼" (5.7cm) strip 44" (111.8cm) long of cotton print fabric
* ✳ One, 9" (22.9cm) square, cotton batting
* ✳ One, 9 ½" (24.1cm) square, cotton print, backing
* ✳ Water-soluble pen
* ✳ DMC floss, red - 321 (3 strands)
* ✳ Double sided fusible web
* ✳ Hand sewing needle

INSTRUCTIONS

1 Print on cardstock and cut out all the lemonade stand pieces.

2 Tape the word pattern "Lemonade 25 cents" onto a window. Tape the white cotton solid piece over the word and trace with a water-soluble pen. Embroider the word using the red DMC floss with a backstitch (see embroidery stitches in the technique section).

3 Follow the instructions in the technique section for sketchy appliqué to cut out all the pieces, overlap the pieces, and place the pieces onto the 8" (20.3cm) square linen piece. Press each piece in place.

4 Machine appliqué using a short straight stitch around each motif with contrasting dark thread as close to the edge as you can, going around each motif twice.

5 Layer and spray baste the jug rug top to the cotton batting piece, and then spray baste the cotton batting piece to the backing piece. Square up the batting and backing piece to the size of the front piece.

6 Bind the jug rug: Use pre-made double fold binding or make your own. To make your own, use a 2 ¼" (5.7cm) strip, approximately 44" (111.8cm) long of a coordinating cotton print. Press the strip in half lengthwise with right side facing out and raw edges lining up. Bind the potholder using your preferred method. I machine stitch my binding to the back and then turn the binding to the front and machine stitch it in place.

Lemonade
25¢

summer

Little Red Riding Hood Doll

I've always loved sewing little dolls for my girls and nieces!
Seeing them cuddle up, carry them around the house, or play
house with them brings me so much joy! This Little Red Riding
Hood Doll is an oversized doll and the perfect size for sitting on
a dresser or bed when she's not being played with!

You will need

* ❋ Doll, cape and apron pattern pieces
* ❋ Fat quarter, red polka dot cotton print, cape and doll head
* ❋ Fat eighth, aqua gingham cotton print, doll body and sleeves
* ❋ One 6 ½" x 11" (16.5 x 27.9cm) rectangle, red stripe cotton print, leggings
* ❋ One, 9" x 11" (22.7 x 27.9cm) rectangle, aqua solid, boots
* ❋ Fat eighth, linen, face and arms
* ❋ One, 7" x 9" (17.8 x 22.9cm) rectangle, wool felt, desired color for hair
* ❋ One, scrap piece, pink wool felt, cheeks
* ❋ One, scrap piece, wool felt, desired color for eyes
* ❋ DMC Floss – Pink, 605, White, Blanc
* ❋ Fat eighth, pink cotton print, apron
* ❋ One, 4" x 38" (10.2 x 96.5cm) strip, white solid, apron tie
* ❋ Two, 16 ½" (41.9cm) long ribbons, hair ribbons
* ❋ Two, 8" (20.3cm) long red ribbons, cape ties
* ❋ Four, crochet and silk flowers, two of each (pre-made from Riley Blake), accent for hair and apron, optional
* ❋ Two buttons, accent for hair and apron, optional
* ❋ One, 16 ½" (41.9cm) long lace, dress trim, optional
* ❋ Fusible web, optional
* ❋ Chop stick or un-sharpened pencil, stuffing tool
* ❋ Poly-fil, stuffing

INSTRUCTIONS

1 Print on cardstock and cut out all the doll, cape and apron pieces. From fabric/felt, cut 2 of the following- head, body, cheek, eyes, pony tail, cape, and apron. Cut 4 of the following- sleeves, arms, leggings, and boots. Cut one of the head and hair.

2 Sew each sleeve to the top of the arm piece right sides together. Sew the top of the boot to the bottom of the legging piece right sides together. Press seams open. Sew the legs and the arms together right sides together using a ¼" (6mm) seam allowance. For extra durability I go around each piece twice, or you can use a zigzag stitch. Leave the top of the arm and legs open for stuffing.

3 Stuff the legs and arms with stuffing using a chopstick or pencil. Leave about a ½" (1.3cm) at the top un-stuffed.

4 Sew the top of the body to the bottom of the head. Place fusible web on the backside of the head, hair, eyes and cheeks (optional). Sew the face onto the head using a small zigzag stitch around the outside edge. Sew the hair on top of the face using a straight stitch. Hand stitch the cheeks with a running stitch, the eyes with a French knot, and the mouth with a backstitch. Sew the crochet flower and silk flower to the top of the hair with a button (optional).

5 Pin the ponytails in place, one on each side of the bottom of the head. Make sure they are lying inward (not outward like they will be when finished). Machine baste the "ponytails" in place with a ⅛" (3mm) seam allowance.

6 Refer to the pattern for arm placement and pin the arms in place on the body. Make sure to place the arms inward on the body when sewing the arms down (not outward like it will be when finished). Machine baste the arms to the body using a zigzag stitch along the raw edges with a ⅛" (3mm) seam allowance.

7 Turn the bottom edge up a ½" (1.3cm) and press. Place the front of the doll right sides together with the back and pin liberally around the edges. Sew a ¼" (6mm) seam allowance around all the edges except the bottom (where the legs go in). Sew around the edges twice for extra durability.

8 Turn the doll right side out and stuff using a chopstick or pencil. Push the stuffing up as much as you can (over stuff) and leave a good amount un-stuffed at the bottom. After the doll is finished you can maneuver stuffing back down to re-distribute the stuffing evenly.

9 Refer to the pattern for the leg placements and carefully pin the legs into the bottom of the body in between the front and back pieces. Pin the bottom of the dress liberally so it is closed. Topstitch the bottom closed sewing slowly and checking the back often to make sure all the layers and legs are stitched together. Hand stitch your lace piece around the bottom of the dress with a running stitch.

Apron

1 Place your apron pieces right sides together and stitch a ¼" (6mm) seam around the sides and bottom. Leave the top open.

2 Turn right side out and press. Topstitch around the sides and bottom. With a large stitch machine baste ¼" (6mm) from the top and then pull the thread to gather the top.

3 Press the white 4" x 38" (10.2 x 96.5cm) strip in half lengthwise so raw edges are lining up. Open, and then press the raw edges to the folded line. Fold in half again and press. Press the end in a ½" (1.3cm) in. Pin the gathered apron piece in the center of the apron ribbon and pin. Topstitch the ribbon closed along the bottom edge.

4 Place the crochet and silk flower on the left side of the apron and hand stitch it with a button to secure it to the apron.

Cape

1 Machine stitch the end of one ribbon to the top left and the other ribbon to the top right edge. Make sure the ribbon is going inward on the cape piece and not outward like it will when finished.

2 Place the cape pieces right sides together and stitch a ¼" (6mm) seam around all the edges leaving a 3" (7.6cm) opening for turning. Turn and then topstitch around all sides.

Oh Deer Wall Quilt

Deer and mushrooms have always been a favorite of mine!
Anything woodland, cute and whimsical catches my fancy! I get to
enjoy these fabulous animals on almost a daily basis as they come
and graze in my yard. Their beauty and wonder always captivates
me no matter how many times they come by for a visit.

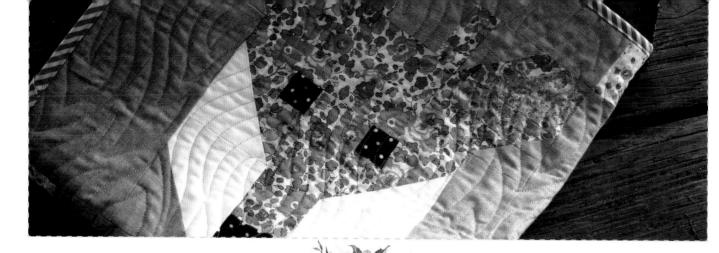

You will need

For One Deer Block (you will be making two):

Low volume floral (deer):

❋ Six, 2 ½" (6.4cm) squares
❋ Four, 1 ½" x 2 ½" (3.8 x 6.4cm) rectangles
❋ Four, 1 ½" (3.8cm) squares
❋ One, 2 ½" x 4 ½" (6.4 x 11.4cm) rectangle
❋ One, 2 ½" x 5 ½" (6.4 x 14cm) rectangle
❋ Two, 2 ½" x 3 ½" (6.4 x 8.9cm) rectangles
❋ One, 1 ½" x 8 ½" (3.8 x 21.6cm) rectangle

Pink Floral Print (ears):

❋ Two, 2 ½" (6.4cm) squares
❋ Six, 1 ½" (3.8cm) squares

White Solid (cheeks):

❋ Two, 3 ½" x 7 ½" (8.9 x 19.1cm) rectangles
❋ One, 1 ½" x 2 ½" (3.8 x 6.4cm) rectangle

Brown Cotton Print (eyes, nose):

❋ Two, 1 ½" (3.8cm) squares
❋ One, 1 ½ x 2 ½" (3.8 x 6.4cm) rectangle

Grey Cotton Solid (background):

❋ Five, 2 ½" (6.4cm) squares
❋ Two, 3 ½" (8.9cm) squares
❋ Two, 2 ½" x 8 ½" (6.4 x 21.6cm) rectangles

For One Mushroom Block (you will be making 8):

Mushroom triangle templates
Floral Cotton Print

❋ One, 3 ³/₈" x 6 ½" (8.6 x 16.5cm) rectangle
❋ Two, 1 ½" x 2 ½" (3.8 x 6.4cm) rectangles

Grey Solid:

❋ Four, 2 ½" (6.4cm) squares

Brown Cotton Print:

❋ Three, 1 ½" x 2 ½" (3.8 x 6.4cm) rectangles

White Solid:

❋ One, 2 ½"(6.4cm) squares
❋ Twelve, 2 ½" x 12 ½" (6.4 x 31.8cm) grey solid rectangles, sashing
❋ Nine, 2 ½" (6.4cm) squares, low volume floral prints, corner stones
❋ One, 32" x 32" (81.3 x 81.3cm) cotton batting
❋ One, 32" x 32" (81.3 x 81.3cm) cotton print, backing
❋ Double fold binding or at least 130" (330.2cm) of 2 ¼" (5.7cm) strips of cotton print to make binding
❋ Basting spray

Deer Block Instructions

1 **Ears:** To make block (a), in the center draw a diagonal line on the wrong side on all four of your 1 ½" (3.8cm) low volume squares. Place two of them right sides together on the right upper corner and one on the left bottom corner on one of the 2 ½" (6.4cm) floral cotton print squares. On your other 2 ½" (6.4cm) floral cotton print squares, place the other two 1 ½" (3.8cm) low volume squares in opposite corners. Sew on the drawn line and then cut a ¼" (6mm) from the seam line and press seams open.

2 To make block (b), and (c), draw a line diagonally the same way in step 1 on all the 1 ½" (3.8cm) floral cotton print squares, and the same with four of the 2 ½" (6.4cm) low volume cotton print squares. Place a 2 ½" (6.4cm) grey solid square and a 2 ½" (6.4cm) low volume square right sides together; sew on the line and then cut a ¼" (6mm) seam from the drawn line. Repeat with the other 3 to make 4 grey/low volume floral print HST's (half square triangles). Place the pink floral 1 ½" (3.8cm) squares on the floral portion of your HST's and sew along those lines, cut a ¼" (6mm) seam and them press. Continue until you have 4 finished.

3 To make block (d), place one of the 1 ½" (3.8cm) pink cotton print squares on the upper left corner of the 2 ½" (6.4cm) low volume cotton print right sides together. Sew along the line, cut a ¼" (6mm) seam and them press seam open. Do the same with your other 1 ½" (3.8cm) pink cotton print square and the 2 ½" (6.4cm) low volume cotton print squares but sew it on the upper right corner.

4 Sew block (a) and (b) together, and sew block (c) and (d) together. Press seams open and then sew those two rows together. Press seams open.

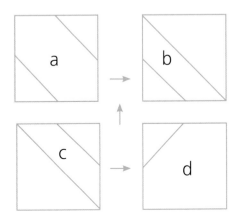

5 **Antlers:** Sew the low volume 1 ½" x 2 ½" (3.8 x 6.4cm) block (e), to the 2 ½" (6.4cm) grey square (f) and then another low volume 1 ½" x 2 ½" (3.8 x 6.4cm) block (g). Press seams open. Then sew that row to the low volume 2 ½" x 4 ½" (6.4 x 11.4cm) rectangle (h). Press seams open.

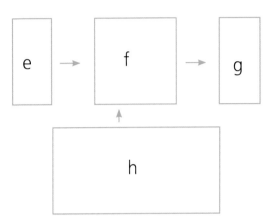

6 **Eyes:** Sew the 1 ½" (3.8cm) brown cotton print (j) to the 1 ½" x 2 ½" (3.8 x 6.4cm) low volume cotton print (k), press seams open. Repeat so you have 2 blocks. Sew one to the left side of the 2 ½" x 3 ½" (6.4 x 8.9cm) low volume cotton print (i), and one to the right side of the other (i) so you have two blocks. Press seams open.

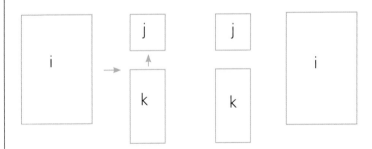

7 On the wrong side of 3 ½" (8.9cm) eye squares (i, j, k) draw a diagonal line. Place on the top of the 3 ½" x 7 ½" (8.9 x 19.1cm) rectangle (l) right sides together. Sew on the line, cut a ¼" (6mm) seam and press seams open. Draw a diagonal line on the two, 3 ½" (8.9cm) grey solid squares (m). Place the 3 ½" (8.9cm) grey solid square (m) on the bottom of the white rectangle (l), and sew along the drawn line. Cut a ¼" (6mm) seam and press seams open. Repeat, but mirror the placement.

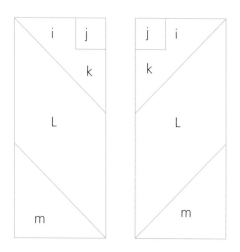

8 **Nose:** Sew the low volume 2 ½" x 5 ½" (6.4 x 14cm) rectangle (n) to the brown 1 ½" x 2 ½" (3.8 x 6.4cm) rectangle (p), and then the white 1 ½" x 2 ½" (3.8 x 6.4cm) rectangle (p). Press seams open. Sew the eye rectangle to the nose rectangle, and then the mirrored eye rectangle. Press seams open.

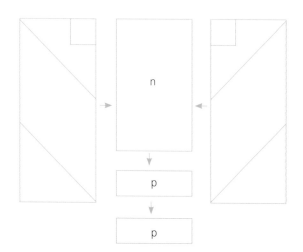

9 Sew the low volume 1 ½" x 8 ½" (3.8 x 21.6cm) rectangle (q) to the eyes and nose pieces. Press seams open. Sew the one grey solid 2 ½" x 8 ½" (6.4 x 21.6cm) rectangle (r) to the left side of the nose and eye pieces and the other grey solid rectangle (s) to the right side of the nose and eye pieces. Sew the left ear to the antler piece, and the right ear to the other side of the antler piece. Press seams open. Finish the block by sewing the ears and antler piece to the eyes and nose piece right sides together and then press seams open.

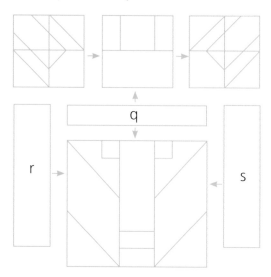

10 Cut another set and repeat steps 1 through 9 to make a second deer block.

Mushroom Block Instructions

1 Draw a diagonal line on two of the grey solid 2 ½" (6.4cm) squares (b, c). Place (b) right side together on the upper left of the 3 ⅜" x 6 ½" (8.6 x 16.5cm) floral cotton print (a), and (c), on the opposite corner. Sew on the drawn line and then cut a ¼" (6mm) seam and press seams open.

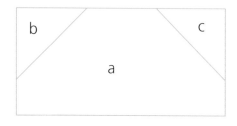

2 Print and cut out the left and right mushroom triangle templates on cardstock. These pieces are the same but mirror each other.

3 Using the mushroom triangle templates, cut out two left mushroom triangles from the 1 ½" x 2 ½" (3.8 x 6.4cm) brown and floral cotton print rectangles. Do the same with the right mushroom triangle templates. Place one floral cotton print triangle right sides together with the brown triangle and sew a ¼" (6mm) seam. Repeat with the other mirrored pieces, and press seams open to create block (d) and (f). Sew block (d) to the 1 ½" x 2 ½" (3.8 x 6.4cm) brown block (e), and then to block (f)

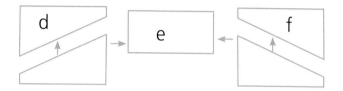

4 Sew the 2 ½" (6.4cm) square grey block (g) to the 2 ½" (6.4cm) square white block (h), and then those to the other 2 ½" (6.4cm) grey block (i). Press seams open. Sew the mushroom top to the middle section and then the middle section to the bottom stem section. Cut seven more of each piece and make seven more mushroom blocks for a total of 8 blocks.

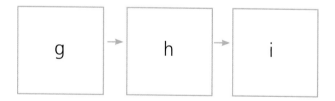

5 Sew four mushroom blocks together into rows of two, and then sew the rows together to have two blocks of four mushrooms.

Finishing the Quilt

1 Arrange the deer and mushroom blocks. Lay out the sashing and corner stone pieces. Machine stitch the blocks to the sashing pieces and the sashing and corner stone pieces to make rows. Machine stitch your rows together.

2 Make a quilt sandwich. Lay out the batting piece. Spray the batting piece with basting spray and then lay your quilt top over the batting piece and hand press so it lays flat. Turn your quilt top and batting over so your batting is facing up and spray your batting with basting spray and then lay your backing piece over the batting and hand press so it lays flat.

3 Hand or machine quilt. I had mine long arm quilted so I was able to skip step 2 (in finishing the quilt) and sent the quilt sandwich pieces to long arm quilter. After it's quilted, trim around the edges of your quilt since the batting and backing pieces are larger.

4 Bind your quilt: Use pre-made double fold binding or make your own. To make your own, attach 2 ¼" (5.7cm) strips of a coordinating cotton print until you have approximately 130" (330.2cm) of binding. Press the strips in half lengthwise with right side facing out and raw edges lining up. Bind the quilt using your preferred method. I machine stitch my binding to the back and then turn the binding to the front and machine stitch it in place.

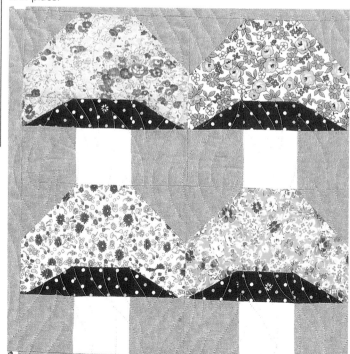

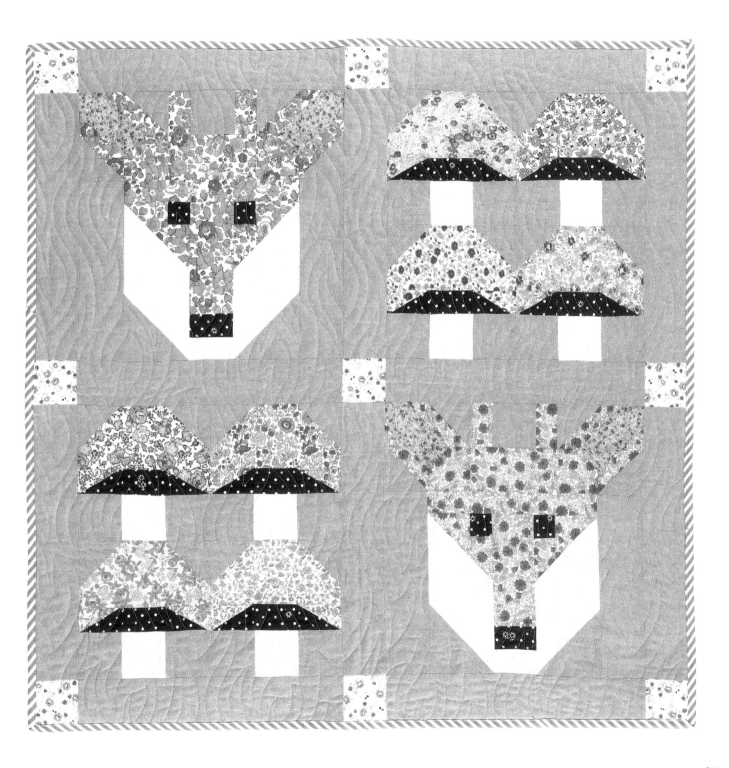

Apple Tree Pillow

In Washington State there is an abundance of apples in the autumn time. This year we even enjoyed picking apples with the family. The kiddos loved climbing the ladders to grab as many apples as they could.

You will need

❋ Eighteen various cotton print scraps, apples

❋ One, cotton print scrap, 18 small leaves

❋ One, 5 ½" x 9" (15 x 22.9cm) rectangle, brown cotton print, tree trunk

❋ One, 20" x 20" (50.8 x 50.8cm) square, linen, background

❋ One, 22" x 22" (55.9 x 55.9cm) square, cotton print, front-back piece

❋ Fusible web

❋ Batting 21" X 21" (53.3 x 53.3cm)

❋ One, 15" x 20" (38.1 x 50.8cm), cotton print, envelope backing

❋ One, 13" x 20" (33 x 50.8cm), cotton print, envelope backing

❋ Basting spray

❋ Double fold binding or at least 85" (215.9cm) of 2 ¼" (5.7cm) strips of cotton print to make binding

INSTRUCTIONS

1 Print the apple, stem and trunk templates onto cardstock. Cut out.

2 Follow the instructions in the technique section for sketchy appliqué to cut out all the pieces using fusible web, and place the pieces onto the 20" (50.8cm) square linen piece. Press each piece in place.

3 Make a quilt sandwich with your pillow top. Spray baste your batting piece, take your 20" x 20" (50.8 x 50.8cm) apple tree block and hand press onto the batting. Turn over and spray baste the other side of batting and hand press the front-back piece to the batting.

4 Machine appliqué using a short straight stitch around each motif with white or contrasting thread (depending on the look you want). I used white thread. Stitch as close to the edge as you can, going around each apple, stem and trunk. Trim the front-back and the batting to the size of the pillow front.

5 To make your envelope backing, fold and press the top edge of your 15" x 20" (38.1 x 50.8cm) cotton print a ½" (1.3cm) down. Then fold it again another ½" (1.3cm) to make a French seam. Stitch two rows, one a ⅛" (3mm) from the edge and another a ¼" (6mm) from that line. Do the same with your second 13" x 20" (33 x 50.8cm) envelope backing piece.

6 Pin the envelope backing pieces with them overlapping to the back of the apple tree pillow front with right sides out. Sew a ⅛" (3mm) seam around the outside edges to secure the envelope backing to the pillow top.

7 Bind the pillow: Use pre-made double fold binding or make your own. To make your own, attach 2 ¼" (5.7cm) strips of a coordinating cotton print until you have approximately 85"(215.9cm) of binding. Press the strips in half lengthwise with right side facing out and raw edges lining up. Bind the quilt using your preferred method. I machine stitch my binding to the back and then turn the binding to the front and machine stitch it in place.

Patchwork Pumpkin & Maple Leaf Placemat

Watching the leaves change colors and picking pumpkins with the family is a couple of my favorites during the autumn! These placemats combine the two to create a fun and easy decoration for your autumn table setting.

You will need

* One, 2 ½" (6.4cm) square, brown cotton print, pumpkin stem
* Four, 2 ½" (6.4cm) squares, low volume cotton print, background
* Eight, 2 ½" (6.4cm) squares, orange cotton print, pumpkin
* Four, 2 ½" (6.4cm) squares, leaf color cotton print, leaf & leaf stem
* Two, 2 ¼" (5.7cm) squares, orange cotton print, pumpkin (for leaf stem square)
* Eight, 3" (7.6cm) squares, orange cotton print, pumpkin (HST's)
* Four, 3" (7.6cm) squares, leaf color cotton print, pumpkin (HST's)
* Four, 3" (7.6cm) squares, low volume cotton print, background (HST's)
* Two, 1 ½" x 10 ½" (3.8 x 26.7cm) strips, low volume cotton print, sashing
* Two, 1 ½" x 12 ½" (3.8 x 31.8cm) strips, low volume cotton print, sashing

* Two, 3 ½" x 12 ½" (8.9 x 31.8cm) strips, natural linen, sides
* Two, 3 ½" x 5" (8.9 x 12.7cm) rectangles, natural linen, pocket lining
* Two, 3 ½" x 5" (8.9 x 12.7cm) rectangles, plaid cotton print, outside pocket
* Two, 2" x 4" (5.1 x 10.2cm) rectangles, orange polka dot print, pocket binding
* One, 7 ½" (19.1cm) square, cotton print, napkin front (child sized)
* One, 7 ½" (19.1cm) square, natural linen, napkin back
* One, 14" x 20" (35.6 x 50.8cm) rectangle of cotton batting
* One, 15" x 21" (38.1 x 53.3cm) rectangle of cotton print, backing
* Double fold binding or at least 68" (172.7cm) of 2 ¼" (5.7cm) strips of cotton print to make binding

INSTRUCTIONS

1 To create the HST's (half square triangles), take one low volume 3" (7.6cm) square and one orange 3" (7.6cm) square. On the wrong side of one of the squares draw a diagonal line from one corner to the opposite corner. Place your other square right sides together with the square you drew your diagonal line on. Machine stitch a ¼" (6mm) away from the line on both sides of the line. Cut on the line so you have two triangles. Press seams open and trim your HST to 2 ½" (6.4cm) square. Repeat with your other 3" (7.6cm) squares so you have four different orange and low volume HST's, and four different orange and leaf color HST's. You will have enough HST's for another placemat so save those for later if you want to make more placemats.

2 For the leaf stem, take the two 2 ¼" (5.7cm) orange squares and draw a diagonal line down the center like you did for the HST's. Place one of the squares on one corner of one of the 2 ½" (6.4cm) leaf color squares. Sew on the line and then cut a ¼" (6mm) away from the line. Press seam open. Place the other 2 ¼" (5.7cm) square on the opposite corner and sew on the line. Cut a ¼" (6mm) away from the line and press seam open.

3 Arrange your 2 ½" (6.4cm) squares and the HST's to make the pumpkin & maple leaf block as in the layout picture. Sew the squares into rows and press seams open. Sew your rows together and press the seams open.

4 Sew the 10 ½" (26.7cm) low volume strips to each side of the pumpkin block. Press seams open. Sew the 12 ½" (31.8cm) low volume strip to the top and bottom of the pumpkin block and press seams open.

5 Spray baste the linen pocket lining to the plaid pocket front. Take the 2" (5.1cm) strip and press in half lengthwise. Sew the raw edge of the strip to the back of the pocket using a ¼" (6mm) seam allowance, fold the binding over to the front and pin in place. Machine stitch as close to the binding edge. Repeat with the other pocket pieces and pocket binding piece.

6 Pin the pocket to the bottom of the 3 ½" x 12 ½" (8.9 x 31.8cm) linen piece. Sew around the pocket edges ⅛" (6mm) to secure it. Repeat with the other pocket piece and 3 ½" x 12 ½" (8.9 x 31.8cm) linen piece. Sew one of the linen/pocket pieces to the right side of the pumpkin block and the other linen/pocket piece to the left side of the pumpkin block.

7 Make a quilt sandwich. Lay out the batting piece. Spray the batting piece with basting spray and then lay your placemat over the batting piece and hand press so it lays flat. Turn your placemat and batting over so your batting is facing up and spray your batting with basting spray and then lay your backing piece over the batting and hand press so it lays flat.

8 Hand or machine quilt. I free motion quilted my placemat with my machine.

9 Bind your placemat: Use pre-made double fold binding or make your own. To make your own, attach 2 ¼" (5.7cm) strips of a coordinating cotton print until you have approximately 68" (172.7cm) of binding. Press the strips in half lengthwise with right side facing out and raw edges lining up. Bind the quilt using your preferred method. I machine stitch my binding to the back and then turn the binding to the front and machine stitch it in place.

10 To make the child sized napkin: Take the 7 ½" (19.1cm) square cotton print and the 7 ½" (19.1cm) linen piece and place them right sides together. Sew a ¼" (6mm) along the outside edges but leave a 3" (7.6cm) opening. Turn the napkin right side out and then topstitch around the outside edges as close to the edge as you can.

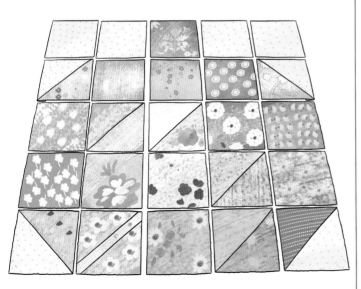

Back to School Pencil Pouch

Back to school time always brings an abundance of shopping for school supplies in my home. We spend many hours going over lists and checking them off as we go to different stores. My kiddos especially love when they can have something homemade to bring to school to organize their supplies. This is a simple and easy project that will be perfect to help organize their pens and pencils. You may even want to make a few so you have some pouches for home too!

You will need

* Two, 1 ½" x 8 ½" (3.8 x 22cm) rectangle, natural linen, background
* One, 8" x 8 ½" (20.3 x 22cm) rectangle, natural linen, background
* Two, 2" X 8 ½" (5.1 x 22cm) rectangle, low volume polka dot print, background of hexagon strip
* One 8 ½" x 13" (22 x 33cm) rectangle, cotton print, lining
* One, 8 ½" x 13" (22 x 33cm) rectangle, cotton batting
* One, 3" (7.6cm) long ribbon/lace, loop
* Lace zipper at least 9" (22.9cm) long
* Sixteen, ½" (1.3cm) hexagon paper templates
* Sixteen, various cotton scraps, hexagons
* Double sided fusible web
* Hand sewing needle

DMC Floss (3 strands each):
* Red - 321
* Aqua - 959
* Pink - 603
* Yellow - 744

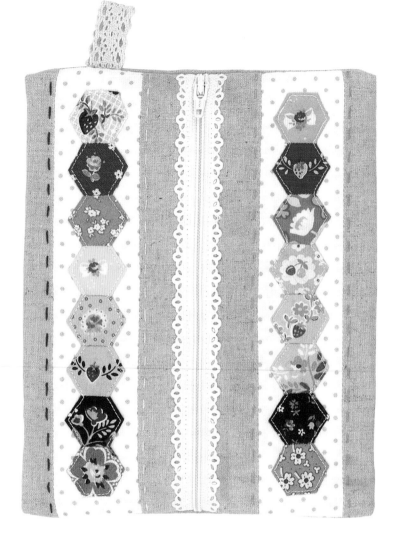

INSTRUCTIONS

1 Print on cardstock and cut out sixteen, ½" (1.3cm) hexagons or use pre-made paper hexagons. Follow the instructions in the Technique section under English Paper Piecing and baste your hexagons. Whip stitch the bottom to the top of the hexagon and make 2 rows of 8. Press the hexagon strips and then remove the basting stitches and paper.

2 Cut out 2 strips of fusible web a little smaller than the hexagon strip. Remove the backside of the paper and place on the back side of the hexagon strips. Remove the other side of the fusible web paper and center the hexagon strips on the 2" x 8 ½" (5.1 x 20.3cm) low volume strips and press. Topstitch the hexagon strips around all the outside edges as close to the edge as you can. I make my stitch length a little smaller on smaller hexagons like these.

3 Sew the left side of one hexagon strip to the long edge of the 1 ½" x 8 ½" (3.8 x 22cm) strip right sides together. Next sew the 8" x 8 ½" (20.3 x 22cm) strip to the right side of the hexagon strip you just stitched right sides together. Add the other hexagon strip on the opposite side of the 8 ½" x 8 ½" (20.3 x 22cm) strip right sides together and then the other 1 ½" x 8 ½" (3.8 x 22cm) linen strip to the other side of the hexagon strip. Press seams open.

4 Spray baste the batting piece and hand press the pencil pouch on top. Place the lining piece on top of the pencil pouch top right sides together. Sew a ¼" (6mm) seam along both the short ends. Turn right side out and press.

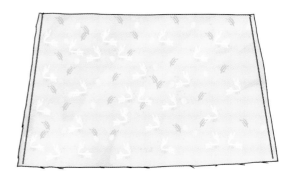

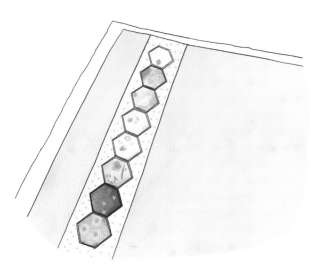

5 Take the ribbon/lace 3" (7.6cm) strip and fold in half so raw edges match up. Place on top of the hexagon strip along the raw edges. Secure the lace loop by sewing along the edge a ⅛" (3mm).

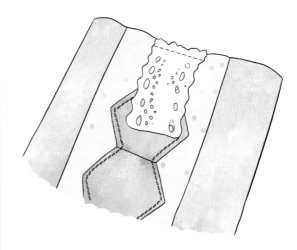

6 Use a running stitch and hand quilt with DMC floss the detail line along the sides of the hexagon strips. I used 4 different colors to add variety.

7 Place the zipper on the top edge of the pencil pouch front and pin in place. Sew ⅛" (3mm) in from the edge to secure the zipper in place. I stitched on the back side so my ¼" (6mm) foot sat right along the edge and easily made a ⅛" (3mm) seam. Also, start with the zipper closed and then unzip the zipper once you get to the zipper handle to move it out of the way. You can use a zipper foot as well to make it easier for stitching on the front side. Make sure you stitch slowly and remove the pins just before you get to them.

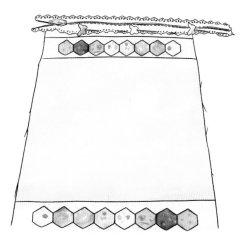

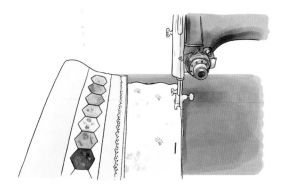

9 Turn inside out and make sure the zipper is in the center of the pouch. Also, make sure the zipper is partially open so you can turn it right side out. Pin in place on the edges. Sew a ¼" (6mm) seam on both edges and then zigzag the edges. Trim the excess zipper. Turn right side out and use a chop stitch to gently push out the corners.

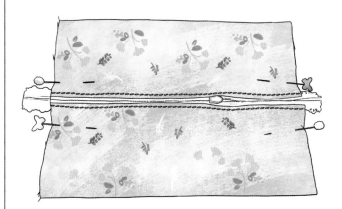

8 Take the opposite edge of the pencil pouch and pin in place. This time, start with the zipper open and stitch the zipper in place by stitching a ⅛" (3mm) seam. Once you get to the zipper, close the zipper so it is not in the way. Again, I stitched mine on the backside since I didn't use a zipper foot.

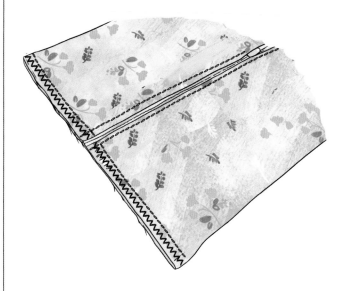

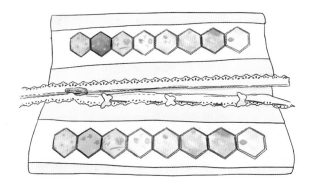

Templates

Cozy Cottage Sewing Machine Cover **22**

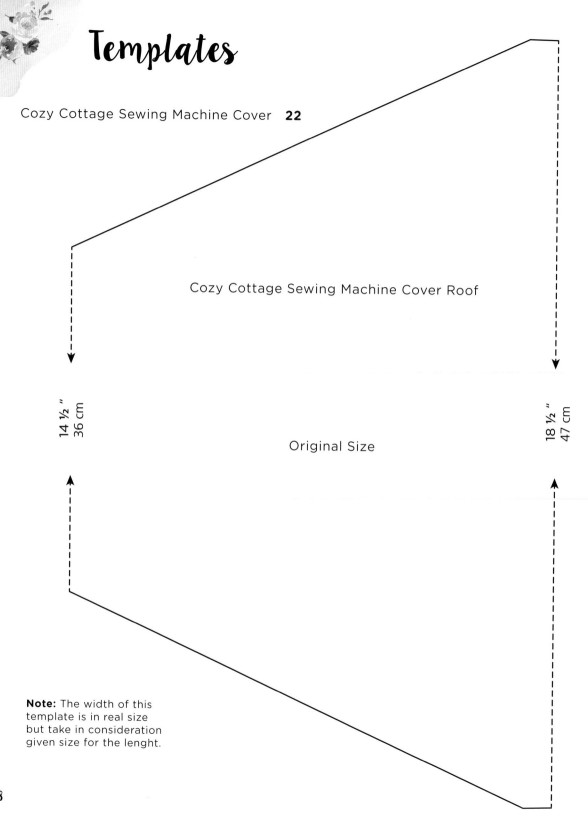

Cozy Cottage Sewing Machine Cover Roof

14 ½ "
36 cm

18 ½ "
47 cm

Original Size

Note: The width of this template is in real size but take in consideration given size for the lenght.

Door

Window

Curtains

Original Size

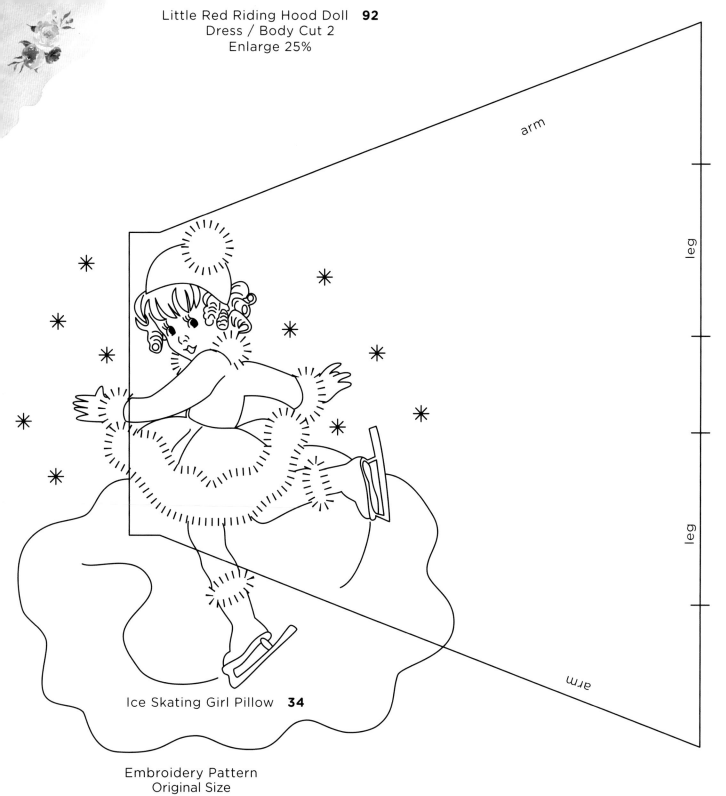

arm

leg

leg

arm

Ice Skating Girl Pillow **34**

Embroidery Pattern
Original Size

Daffodil

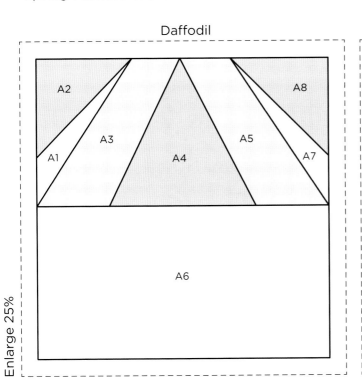

Enlarge 25%

Daffodil Leaves

Enlarge 25%

Tulip

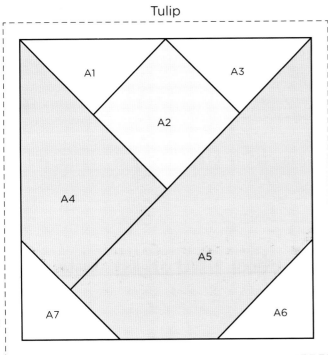

Enlarge 25%

Tulip Leaves

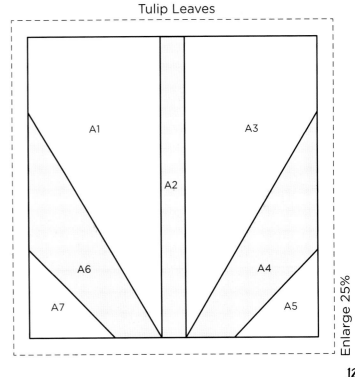

Enlarge 25%

Garden Apron **48**

Cross Stitch Pattern

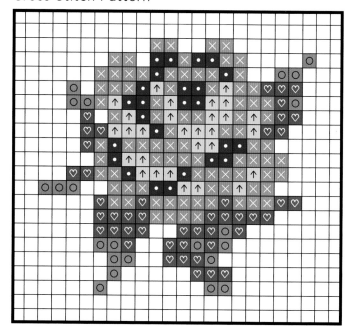

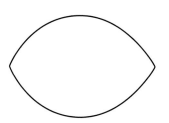

Original Size

Stranded Cotton (Art 117)

⬛	304	♥	701	
✕	603	⚫	704	
↑	963			

Strawberry Patchwork Bag **78**

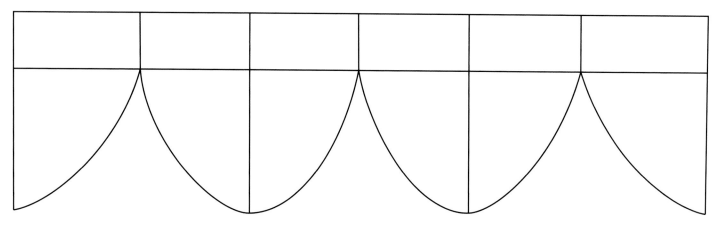

Enlarge 67%

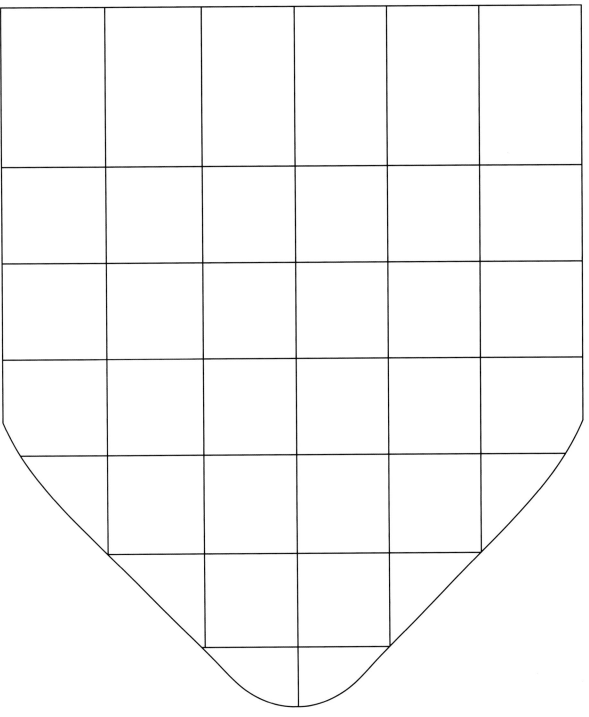

Enlarge 200%

Patchwork Market Tote **70**
Embroidery Pattern

Market Day!

Original Size

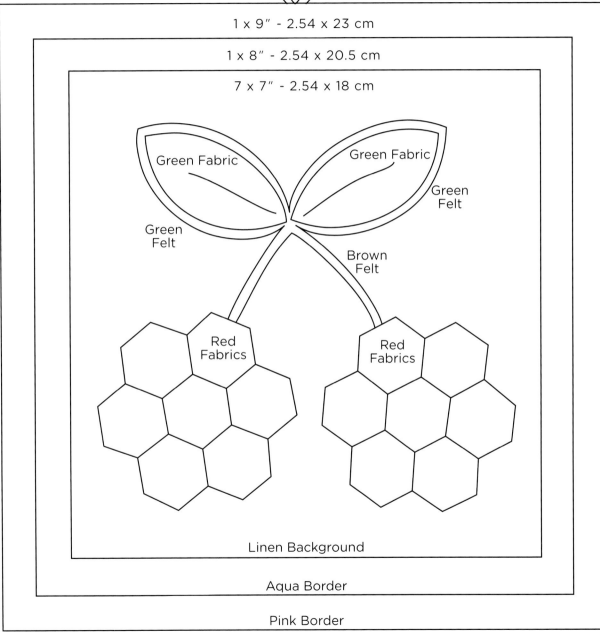

Loop

1 x 9" - 2.54 x 23 cm

1 x 8" - 2.54 x 20.5 cm

7 x 7" - 2.54 x 18 cm

Green Fabric

Green Fabric

Green Felt

Green Felt

Brown Felt

Red Fabrics

Red Fabrics

Linen Background

Aqua Border

Pink Border

Enlarge 25%

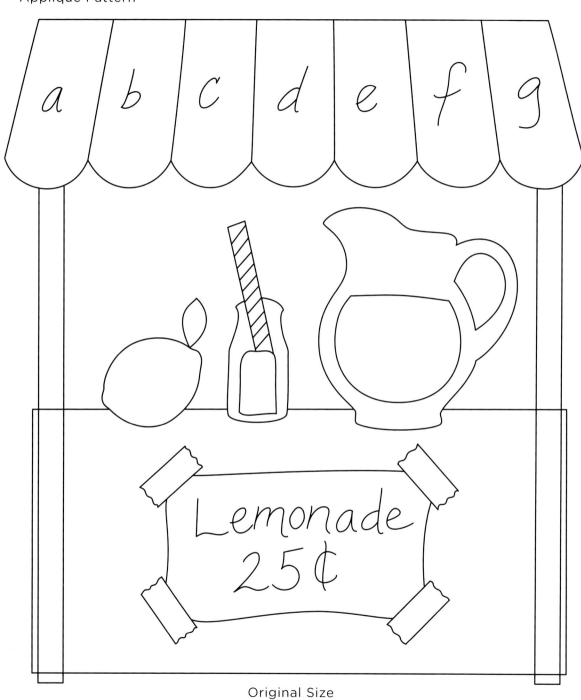

a b c d e f g

Lemonade
25¢

Original Size

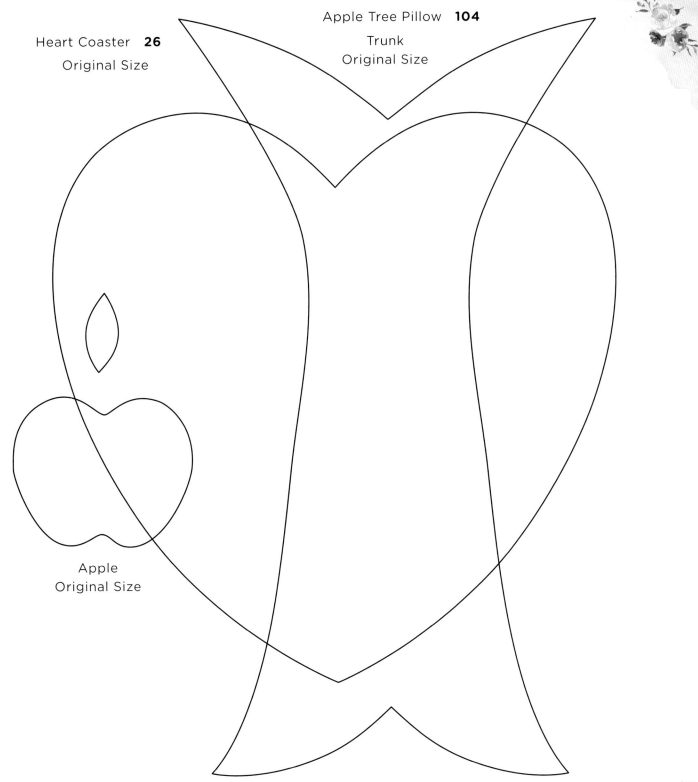

Heart Coaster **26**
Original Size

Apple Tree Pillow **104**
Trunk
Original Size

Apple
Original Size

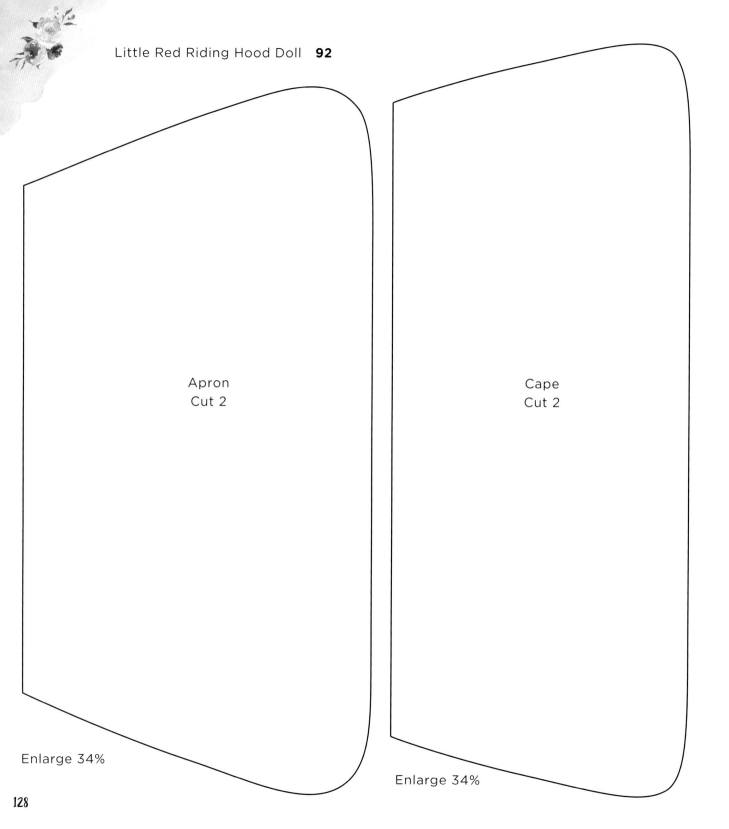

Apron
Cut 2

Cape
Cut 2

Enlarge 34%

Enlarge 34%

Little Red Riding Hood Doll **92**

Head
Cut 2

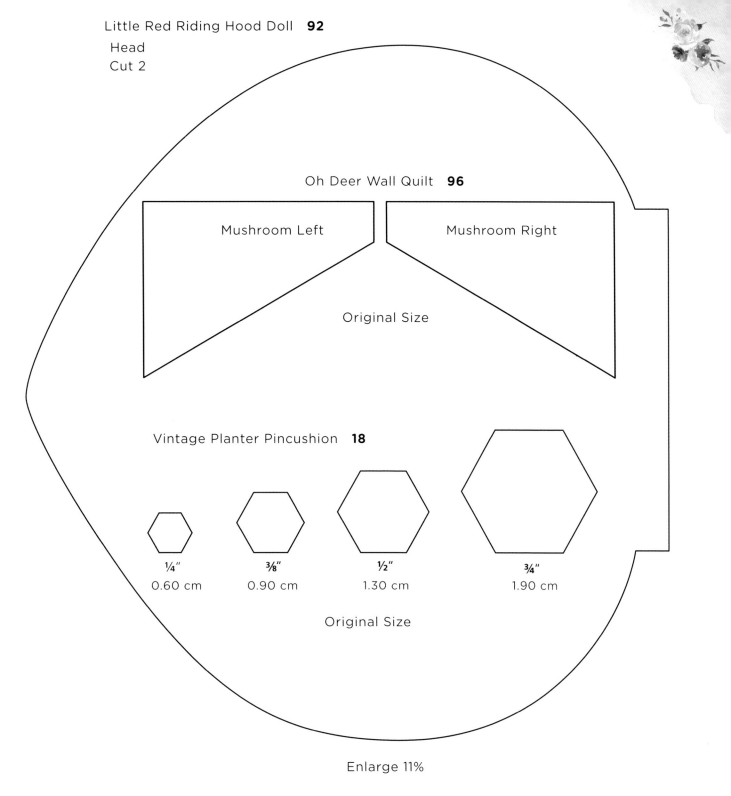

Oh Deer Wall Quilt **96**

Mushroom Left

Mushroom Right

Original Size

Vintage Planter Pincushion **18**

¼"
0.60 cm

⅜"
0.90 cm

½"
1.30 cm

¾"
1.90 cm

Original Size

Enlarge 11%

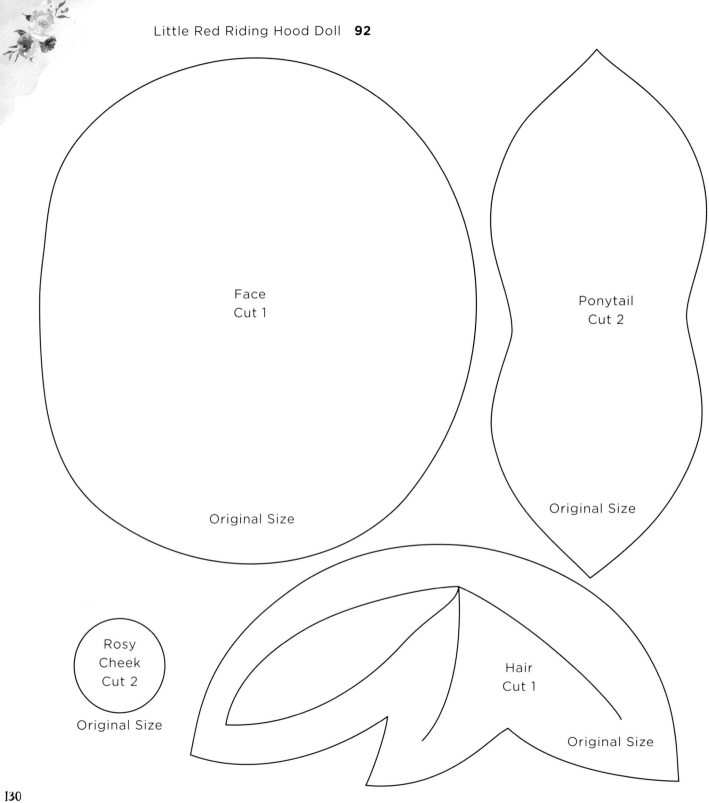

Face
Cut 1

Original Size

Ponytail
Cut 2

Original Size

Rosy
Cheek
Cut 2

Original Size

Hair
Cut 1

Original Size

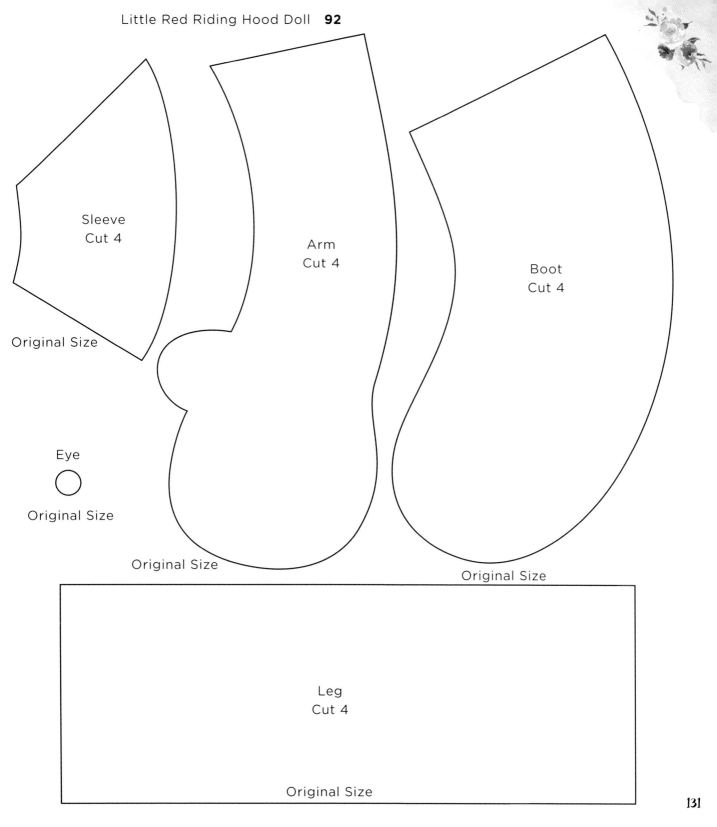

Sleeve
Cut 4

Original Size

Arm
Cut 4

Boot
Cut 4

Eye

Original Size

Original Size

Original Size

Leg
Cut 4

Original Size

Resources and Acknowledgments

Choosing beautiful fabric and supplies can be such a joy at the beginning of each project! There are so many places that offer a wide selection that sometimes it can be hard to know where to go. Here are a list of some of my favorite places to acquire new fabrics and supplies for my stash and projects.

A special thanks to Riley Blake Designs for contributing fabric for several projects!

FABRIC SHOPS

Westwood Acres
The perfect place to go when you are looking for pre-cuts and bundles!

www.westwoodacresfabric.com

Polka Dot Tea
An Australian online fabric store with a fabulous selection including Japanese and Liberty fabrics!

www.etsy.com/shop/PolkaDotTeaFabrics

Whimsy Quilts & Fabrics
A great selection of beautiful floral, whimsical and modern fabrics!

http://www.whimsyquiltsandfabrics.com/

Gooba Designs
Here you will find a great variety of Moda and Cotton + Steel fabrics!

www.etsy.com/shop/GoobaDesigns

Jo-Ann Fabric & Craft
I get many supplies at Jo-Ann craft store.
Some of them are:
Cotton batting, thread, lace zippers, basting spray (online only for the 505 spray), rotary cutter and mat and many more.

Long Arm Quilter
For long arm quilting I recommend the talented Vickey of Studio V.
She did a fabulous job long arm quilting the "Oh Deer Quilt", and the "Pretty Pinwheels on Point Quilt".
http://www.studiovquilting.com

Thanks to Hilal Baltacı- the blogger behind CafeCraftIstanbul for letting us taking beautiful photography in her house.